INTENSIVE CARE

꧁꧂

CUIDADOS INTENSIVOS

ARTURO GUTIÉRREZ PLAZA

TRANSLATED FROM THE SPANISH
BY ARTHUR DIXON

FOREWORD BY MIGUEL GOMES

𝒜
'Alliteratïon

INTENSIVE CARE | ARTURO GUTIÉRREZ PLAZA
First edition in English in June 2020
Translated from the Spanish by Arthur Dixon

© Arturo Gutiérrez Plaza
© For the foreword: Miguel Gomes
© Alliteratïon Publishing, 2020

Design by Elisa Barrios
Cover by Andrea Martínez

"Dedication" by Czeslaw Milosz, translated by the author,
from *The Collected Poems: 1931-1987*, The Ecco Press, 1988.
"Nothing Twice" by Wislawa Szymborska, translated by Stanislaw
Baranczak and Clare Cavanagh, from *View with a Grain of Sand: Selected
Poems*, Harcourt, Brace & Company, 1995.

ISBN: 978-1-7378537-3-2

TRANSLATOR'S NOTE

The poems that make up *Intensive Care* have lived through a long convalescence. In keeping with its central comparison between the care required by poems and the care required by patients, this bilingual edition went through various treatments, was transferred from one ward to another, and was examined by a number of specialists before finally being discharged.

I met Arturo Gutiérrez Plaza in Fall 2013 as an undergraduate in his Spanish American literature class at the University of Oklahoma, and it didn't take long for us to become not only *tocayos* but also friends. I spent the Spring 2014 semester in Granada, Spain, where my latent infection with the translation bug developed into a full-blown case. Back in Oklahoma, I met up with Arturo at Café Plaid, a classic university hangout spot that has sadly since closed. There, he handed me a signed copy of *Cuidados intensivos*, in the hopes that its poems would someday be read in English.

I happily accepted the mission. I wrote my first drafts of the English-language poems that now form *Intensive Care* by hand in college-ruled notebooks. One of my first translations from the book, "If You Let Me," was a hit at a "cover slam" hosted at Second Wind, a non-profit coffee shop on Norman, Oklahoma's much-loved Campus Corner. In Fall 2015, I collaborated with my friend and professor Grady

Wray, completing translations of all the poems and writing a bilingual essay on the translation process. Little did we know, this process was far from over.

I left Oklahoma again in Spring 2016, this time for Puebla, Mexico, where I worked with Marcelo Rioseco— dedicatee of "Oklahoma Nocturne"—on the planning phase of the journal *Latin American Literature Today* (LALT), and with Carolina Rueda on the film *Oklahoma Mon Amour*, which features my finest attempts at acting, along with subtitles translated into Spanish by Arturo himself. Upon my return from Mexico, Daniel Simon, Editor in Chief of LALT's sister publication *World Literature Today* (WLT), suggested that we publish a couple of Arturo's poems in this prestigious journal. In September 2016, "The Ant" and "Universidad-Indios Verdes" were the first poems from *Intensive Care* to see the light of day in English through the print and digital pages of WLT.

I proceeded to graduate school at the University of Oklahoma, still revising Arturo's poems, always hoping for a chance to publish the collection in its entirety and thereby complete the treatment program we had started back at Café Plaid when I was a mere undergrad. That chance arrived in 2020 thanks to Alliteratïon and the invaluable editorial work of Garcilaso Pumar.

The final phase of this collection's treatment was much different from the first. Arturo and I no longer discussed the poems in person over coffee; this time we used Google Duo, he in Caracas, Venezuela and I in Tulsa, Oklahoma, both stuck indoors due to the pandemic that is currently shaking our world and that will surely leave it a different place than before: COVID-19, the novel coronavirus, a disease that has pushed us further apart and brought us closer together all at once. Before we settled into the task of revising the poems one last time, Arturo told me about the strict quarantine and the empty streets of Caracas. But, of course, Caracas is used to curfews and dangers waiting outside your door. Our conversation left me thankful for health and safety wherever we can find it, and hopeful for a time when our neighbors, in Venezuela and everywhere else, can step outside their homes without fear.

In "Watering Hole," the fragmentary *ars poetica* with which *Intensive Care* concludes, Arturo puts a twist on a line by fellow Venezuelan poet Eugenio Montejo: *"Creo que no creo."* Without further context, the meaning of this sentence is ambiguous—in Montejo's poem, we understand that its two conjugated verbs represent the same word, *"creer,"* "to believe," and the poem becomes a reflection on the difficulties of faith. Arturo adds context and changes this understanding, revealing that the second *"creo"* refers not to *"creer"* but to *"crear"*: *"Creo que no creo. Tan solo escribo sin copia del original."* "I believe I do not create. I just write without a copy of the original." With this recognition of the unending game of influence, homage, and extrapolation that characterizes his own work, Arturo captures a greater truth about literature, and maybe all art, and maybe everything we ever say: at the end of the day, every "original" poem is a translation of something. Every word comes from somewhere and has somewhere to go.

I am grateful to Arturo for giving me the chance to help these words keep moving across linguistic and national borders, and to all the friends I've mentioned who have helped care for them along the way. I wish them good health in these uncertain times, and safe travels to their next destination. I am sure—and happy—that it won't be the last.

Arthur Dixon
Tulsa, Oklahoma
March 2020

POETRY AND *PATHOS*

This book's title suggests a vocation, an attitude toward language, and oblique reflections that address human fate as much as the most tangible transformations of the poet's country. This discreet phenomenology is hemmed in by *pathos*—passion and sickness—and by a rigorous watchfulness.

VOCATION

Intensive Care is a lyrical autobiography in which Arturo Gutiérrez Plaza, the individual, takes little part. Baudelaire and Whitman cultivated this genre, which demands, as Lawrence Lipking pointed out, that the poet be transformed into a mask and "purified by his words," far from the man, whether famous or unknown, who gave rise to him[1]. This collection's titular poem itself operates in the area of a certain intimacy, like that which is evoked in its first stanza:

---

[1]   Lawrence Lipking, *The Life of the Poet: Beginning and Ending Poetic Careers*, Chicago: UCP, 1984, p. 164.

My siblings don't read poetry,
my parents didn't either.
By dictate of the present day
my children strengthen
this tradition, now familiar, at school.

Said intimacy is immediately supplanted by an inverse,
desanctifying revelation:

And then poetry lays us bare:
it sarcastically reveals a fatal ailment.

(Words also convalesce
under everyday wonder.)

And in the end, the hybrid creature—half poet, half poem—
must submit to metonymic "purification" in which the
human part ends up replaced by the language part, with
some help, of course, from prosopopoeia:

But if the matter is prolonged,
if the malady stretches further,
for your own good and your people's peace
seek out other extreme unctions:

admit the poem to intensive care.

It should be noted, nonetheless, that the triumph of language
over the individual also implies an unexpected and paradoxi-
cal triumph over dehumanization, because words have become
the vehicle of a new communal experience, in line with the one
described in the best modern lyric poetry by Theodor Adorno[2]:

2   *Notes to Literature*, Shierry Weber Nicholsen tr., New York: Columbia UP,
1991, vol. 1: pp. 42-45.

the identity of the "I" with which the composition begins is broadened, toward the halfway point, into a "we," and by the conclusion it has become a "you" that enters into dialogue with incessant crystallizations of subjectivity in the suffering space of the poem (wracked with inversions, impossibilities, latent oxymorons: triumphal suffering; the longed-for harbor that becomes the last, decisive word, in whose silence poetry begins).

LANGUAGE

In this book, language is presented as an objective form of our experience. The poem represents the threshold between introspection and a phenomenic horizon constantly brushed against by signs. The composition titled "Portico" offers the key:

> Every day, nighttime cultivates
> a flat white plot
>   in which to plant the poem.

> It senses the sprouts,
>   attentive
>   to the passing of the seasons.

> Maybe it'll come in by the fall.

> Sometimes flowers bloom at the wrong time.

The poem's time is the word's crop; at least, this is the implication of the last line, which brings together and concentrates the two semantic fields between which the images have been debating: the first is the field of vegetation and of man's interaction with it—*cultivates, to plant, sprouts*; the second is the field of time invested with the cosmos: *every day, seasons, fall.* The final line is the soil in which these fields take root in order to then bloom in a universe outside natural rules. The law of the poet is the search for such syntheses. This should not lead us to believe that Gutiérrez Plaza favors the intellectualism of a few great twentieth-century poets like António Ramos Rosa[3], who, in verse collections like *Sobre o Rosto da Terra* [On the face of the earth], *Ocupação do Espaço* [Occupation of space], *Terrear* [Earthify], and *Quando o Inexorável* [When the inexorable], made a cosmogonic source of writing:

Caminho um caminho de palavras
(porque me deram o sol)
e por esse caminho me ligo ao sol
e pelo sol me ligo a mim

***

E porque a noite não tem limites
alargo o dia e faço-me dia
e faço-me sol porque o sol existe

***

Mas a noite existe
e a palavra sabe-o[4]

---

3   António Ramos Rosa (1924-2013) was a Portuguese poet, translator, and visual artist.

4   "I walk along a path of words / (because the sun gave them to me) / and along this path I tie myself to the sun / and along the sun I tie myself to myself / *** / And because the night has no limits / I widen the day and make myself day / and I make myself sun because the sun exists / *** / But the night exists / and the word knows it".

While not lacking in rational charms, these fragments from *Sobre o Rosto da Terra*, in which adanism gives rise to a neo-sophistic rhetoric, are situated at an expressive and ideological pole almost totally opposite that of *Intensive Care*. The attitude captured in many passages of Gutiérrez Plaza's poetry comes closer to that of Eugenio Montejo[5] in *Alfabeto del mundo* [Alphabet of the world] or *Fábula del escriba* [Fable of the scribe], where the relationship with the cosmos is receptive, preservative: the one who "notes down" is integrated into a continuum that eliminates the difference between object and subject. No titanism or psychic inflations here: the lyric voice of *Intensive Care* leaves no room for doubts, such that the reader amalgamates this voice with the "night" it invokes. In the last line, the impersonal act of "blooming" wipes out the temptation toward self-deification that brushes against Ramos Rosa's speaker, just as it brushed against—to add another memorable name to a poetic family that is truly quite large—the speakers of Vicente Huidobro[6].

Gutiérrez Plaza's language is not the palace of the "little god," of Adam, or of the hero; if it can be linked to anything, it is to an askesis, or a series of tentative approximations of a person who does not know himself (that is to say, a person who is not omniscient) and, therefore, can only strive to find himself:

I write like a monk who denies
his incredulity and prays with blind faith [...]

My task is to excavate unknown poems,
to dig tunnels and passageways
in the hope of stumbling into splendid galleries [...]

---

5   Eugenio Montejo (1938-2008) was a Venezuelan poet and essayist.

6   Vicente Huidobro (1893-1948) was a Chilean poet and the founder of the literary movement known as Creationism.

At night I catch no glimpse of the Holy Grail.
Nevertheless, I persist,
I seek to repair its reliquary,
to keep watch
over the source of dreams. ("The Reliquary")

The agonism of the figure who humbly notes down the universe, the "scribe," can sometimes be observed in certain Montejian motifs that Gutiérrez Plaza employs consciously, like that of the "scream" of the bird in which the poet is also torn apart. More subtly, it makes itself known in the secret of the being corralled in darkness, especially when the poem's last line foretells a brilliant liberation: "They say you'll be back soon, / and the sky, bit by bit, will start to clear" ("And You Seem to Smile"). The scribe's radical anguish can also be sensed in the systematic violation of mimesis, like the one proposed in "Behindtime," a refined homage not only to Montejo, but also to Cubism and its preferences, already latent in a poet who, as we have seen, can pass from the "I" to the "we" to the "you" in a single poem, undoing monumental or immovable identities or perspectives, convincing us in the least argumentative way possible that language is a poor instrument for capturing reality, but is the most apt of instruments, without a doubt, for materializing our struggle to understand it and belong to it.

FATE

If one speaks of "struggles" in the poetry of Gutiérrez Plaza, one must not omit, logically, the struggle that most affects the individual, because it erases him: that of mortality. This struggle, still, translates painful intimacy into certainty of a future in which the "I" meets its fate of dissolving into a vast otherness.

The process begins with what is perhaps its tipping point: the materiality of the goodbye bid to everyone and to everything, the "Last Words" that are, in fact, the first words of the book. Immediately after, we land on the theme of the disappearance of the point of origin, with elegiac lines that evoke the dying moments of the mother, whom the poetic voice, in turn, imagines departing with the nostalgia of her own origin, "sheltered in your father's music" ("In You").

This fleeting, while undeniably powerful, *mise en abyme* is reformulated more serenely in other poems like "Meditation on the Future," where "the virtue of abysses" can be glimpsed, if only barely, or "Knowledge," where the sensation of loss is inserted, with no aura of tragedy, into a cosmic order that guarantees not a happy ending, but rather the acceptance of even emptiness itself through song:

...And the birds

I listen to them again
like one who knows
that something is already lost
forever

The raw material seems to retain an imprint of Orphic myth, traces of its not-yet-scattered signs: the ellipses with which the poem begins link the here-and-now of the word to an immemorial, cyclical past—like natural rhythms, "again"—that nourishes us with the unsolvable riddle of a certain prescience.

Loss is the driving force behind a good measure of these poetics and, not by chance, the same can be said of the two real poets mentioned in the book who are, in a way, also "characters" in the fictional world that is drafted from one poem to another, especially when we read "Reverón, Macuto-New York (MoMA 2007)": our already-recalled

Montejo and Pedro Lastra[7]. The questioning of a ghostly Reverón activates the presence of the absent. Additionally, the poem alludes to one of the most traumatic moments of recent Venezuelan history: the 1999 landslides on the Caribbean coast, which, besides causing thousands of deaths, destroyed a part of Venezuela's cultural memory:

> What's left of where you lived, what's left of your Castillete.
> Here, now, in this city, the white of your canvas
> hides not just the color of our tropics,
> the incessant sound of their palm tree forests.
>
> Now it's the light of an overexposed photo,
> the one in which we once were but no longer,
> erased by an avalanche of mud and death.

The physiology of poems like this one is governed, to a large extent, by the *ubi sunt*. Here, its nostalgic call is reinforced by superimposing geographical and temporal distance between the present of enunciation and the communion of friendship over the physical disappearance of a place heavy with spirit.

The travel poems that abound in the book, in the finest vein of Enrique Lihn[8]—it is no accident that the first epigraph comes from his *Diario de muerte* [Diary of death]—contribute to expanding and nuancing the vision of a fate marked by scarcity and loss. Perhaps the harshest configuration of these poems can be glimpsed in "The Foreigner," where the subtraction of presence is affirmed with no need for the production of a physical absence.

With that, let us leave behind the realm of metaphysics to enter the realm of ethics.

---

7   Pedro Lastra (1932-) is a Chilean poet and essayist.

8   Enrique Lihn (1929-1988) was a Chilean poet, playwright, and novelist.

Venezuela comes before us with its swollen pride, its gobs of spit, its ticks, its sewers, and its underground wretched. "Citizenship," "In a Metro Station Not Seen by Pound (in Caracas, not Paris)," "Extract from the Book of Saints of the Good Revolutionary," "The Militiaman," and other poems paint its portrait.

This is not *political poetry*, in the worst sense of the label. It is, rather, an attentive but intuitive examination of place that comes in contact with subjectivity in the discourses received from the sphere of power. The "sermon," the "diatribe," the "order" stand in contrast to the graffiti, the fragments of voices that emerge from the newspaper (a masterpiece: "Refuse to Defend Good Manners"). Above all, they stand in contrast to silence: material silence as much as the silence of unravelled reason in absurd verbal proliferation that does not fit with the character's diluted voice, as emerges in the anomic emptiness of "Two Homelands." In this poem's title, there is a provocation, an intertextual subversion of the figures of poets as martyrs and heroes, since its lines suggest a homeland that, out of an excess of conceptual manhandling, winds up dissolved:

> That's what people are like!
> They prick up their ears,
> they gossip,
> they hide behind the ferns.

> Someone passes and says
>   what they say.

> They lift up slogans,
> they flap their wings
>   birds of ill omen.

They're only whispers,
things that don't happen.

Gutiérrez Plaza's oppressive, tragic country differs relatively little from the country that reappears in the work of various significant poets of his generation or the one preceding it, who bore witness, from 1989 on, to the failure of Venezuelan modernity, or at least to the failure of the version of this modernity that was elaborated by official media starting in the mid-twentieth century. The intensification of this collapse in the new millenium, with a regression to the nation's origins meticulously imposed through the pro-independence mythology preached from the altars of Chavismo, shines through also in poetry that interrogates reality. Truly miraculous is the fact that *Intensive Care* responds with renewed faith to the vacuous collectivism that reigns in public life. This results, still, from Eros and the interior worlds he helps create. Communions and enigmas, untranslatable into "slogans," are preferred over the wars and epics of fossilized heroes; justice and equality are, in this case, affective. Only rarely has Venezuelan poetry succeeded in achieving an emotional verisimilitude so discreet, so genuine, as the one we perceive, for example, in "Between Hands":

When they come together to pray
they beg for an end to resentment.
Meanwhile, if they conspire
—make pacts and touch—
they distribute the caresses
of a single body,
the one that shapes their desires.
Together they weigh up a fortunate mystery.
They recognize each other and do business with eternity.

The conspiracy is not only carnal, because the "hand," of course, brings us back to reflections on the questions of vocation and purpose: back to a meditation on language. For this reason, the book ends with "Watering Hole," an *ars poetica* that does not cease to be a poem, and that runs into the sea of analogies: "These days, like patients in care, also words." This comparison is admirable in that it avoids allegories—that is to say, sermons—and in that it flows through numerous interpretations, freed of any doctrine, that do not declare who the doctor is, what the disease is, or if the sickness's outcome will be joyful or fatal. The task of answering these questions is entrusted to the reader.

Intensive Care is an absolutely realized book, lucid, always moving, full of suggestions that hit the target of imagination. Its thematic matrices evolve, complement each other, and are finally fused in a glimpse of the mystery to which the poet aspires. In said mystery, that which has been scattered or split is reconstituted. This is both a book and a repertoire that contains the varied registers of a poet's writing, almost a treatise on the possibilities of the lyric voice. With it, the author offers us a testament to his serene commitment to giving words the care they deserve.

Miguel Gomes

INTENSIVE CARE

CUIDADOS INTENSIVOS

There exists an ugly likelihood that the fear of dying
and the despair of death are
normally as inseparable as the fingernail and the flesh.

ENRIQUE LIHN

I will feel lost,
Unhappy and at home.

SEAMUS HEANEY

With smiles and kisses, we prefer
to seek accord beneath our star,
although we're different (we concur)
just as two drops of water are.

WISLAWA SZYMBORSKA

What is poetry which does not save
Nations or people?
A connivance with official lies,
A song of drunkards whose throats will be cut in a moment,
Readings for sophomore girls.

CZESLAW MILOSZ

LOBBY WITHOUT COUCH

ANTESALA SIN DIVÁN

Últimas palabras

No será por estos lados
donde se inicien las despedidas.

La memoria es vertical
y si vivimos de pie
lo hacemos
por confiar en sus sombras.

En un principio hubiera bastado
acudir a una escena familiar:
el padre monologaba en la mesa,
la madre sorbía su sopa,
los hijos asentían.
Cada quien levantaba murallas
para proteger sus fronteras.
Se abovedaban en el rencor.

Puertas adentro, sin embargo, acaecía otra historia.

En el lugar del viento había una casa cordial,
un sitio donde no hacía falta renunciar a la inocencia.
Allí vivíamos bajo el amparo de una diáfana soledad.

"No, no será aquí" —repetían incipientes ventiscas,
no será aquí donde oigamos decir las últimas palabras.

Ya se fueron la culpa y los culpables,
no hay transeúntes
y se hace tarde.

Ya pronto nos iremos sin decir adiós.

Last Words

The goodbyes won't start
around here.

Memory is vertical
and if we live standing up
we do so
because we trust in its shadows.

At first it would have been enough
to refer to a familiar scene:
the father gives a monologue at the table,
the mother slurps her soup,
the kids nod.
They all build walls
to protect their borders.
They lock themselves away in resentment.

Indoors, though, another story takes place.

In the place of the wind there was a cozy house,
a site where there was no need to give up on innocence.
There we lived in the shelter of a see-through solitude.

"No, it won't be here," repeated incipient blizzards,
It won't be here where we hear the last words.

The guilt and the guilty have already left,
there are no innocent bystanders
and it's getting late.

Before long we'll leave without saying goodbye.

Cuando no era

A Rafa Davis

Ha creído verme cruzando
el jardín del fondo, del limonero a la mampara
de la sala.

JOSÉ WATANABE

Se han ido tantos sin haber costumbre.

Unos pernoctaron, pasivos, en el dolor,
otros, sin girar la vista, tomaron
por el camino recto hasta dar con el país
donde es fecundo el olvido.

Tantos han partido cuando no era,
que cuesta no verlos a diario,
merodeando entre nosotros,
entrando y saliendo de nosotros,
cruzando sin permiso y a escondidas
las esquinas más húmedas, las más oscuras.

Se fueron y aquí quedamos.

Se fueron pero no sus voces
que aún nos hablan sin preguntar
¿quién está donde se estaba,
dónde el sueño o cuándo la partida comenzó?

Se fueron y una mano toca la puerta.

When They Shouldn't Have

To Rafa Davis

He thought he saw me crossing
the back garden, from the lemon tree to the partition
of the living room.
JOSÉ WATANABE

So many have left, we're unaccustomed.

Some spent the night, passive, in pain,
others, looking neither right nor left, set off
down the straight path until they reached the country
where forgetfulness is fertile.

So many departed when they shouldn't have,
it's hard not to see them every day,
prowling around us,
entering and exiting us,
crossing the dampest and the darkest corners
without permission, hidden.

They left and here we stay.

They left, but not their voices
which still speak to us without asking:
Who is where one was?
Where's the dream? When did the game begin?

They left and a hand knocks on the door.

Urgido en ti

No sé si avivaste el tañido de las campanas,
si ya, desde el amanecer, tu sonrisa
había raptado las desavenencias del cielo
o si se aposentó un pájaro azul
para ahuyentar las aves grises
que hasta ayer coronaban las cornisas.

Sólo sé que en tus últimas cuatro horas
te besé,
te lo dije mucho —como nunca— "te quiero"
y te repetí, te susurré al oído
mientras te adormilaban,
—aún incrédulo— la única plegaria que aprendí
en estos treinta días imperecederos:
"Mamá, ya vas a mejorar,
los doctores dicen que saldrás,
pronto les dirás adiós a los cuidados intensivos".

Te lo repetí día a día, apreté tus manos
henchidas de antibióticos,
aparté las sondas para decírtelo
mientras te adormecían a las puertas del gran sueño.

"Sepsis" afirmaba el acta final
pero yo insistía
te repetía lo mucho
te repetía "te quiero"
hasta sepultar con prisa
(ante el minutero) mis miedos,
mis querellas, mis resentimientos.

In You

I don't know if you brightened the ringing of the bells,
if already, since sunrise, your smile
had captured the disputes of the sky
or if a blue bird perched
to frighten off the gray ones
that crowned the ledges until yesterday.

I only know that in your last four hours
I kissed you,
I told you more times than ever before "I love you"
and I repeated, I whispered in your ear
as they made you sleep,
still incredulous, the only prayer I learned
in those thirty everlasting days:
"Mamá, you're going to get better,
the doctors say they'll let you go,
soon you'll say goodbye to intensive care."

I said it to you day after day, I squeezed your hands,
swollen from the antibiotics,
I moved the tubes aside to tell you
as they sent you to sleep at the doors of your long rest.

"Sepsis" proclaimed the final report
but I insisted
I repeated so much
I repeated "I love you"
until I quickly buried
(before time ran out) my fears,
my complaints, my bitterness.

En tus últimas cuatro horas
de vida
todo se hizo útero
mientras te fugabas anidada en la luz,
amparada en la música de tu padre.

Y cuando en la máquina sabionda
vencieron los ceros
cerré tus ojos
y lloré con el llanto urgente
de la primera vez,
cuando perdido, arrojado
en el mundo busqué tu mirada.

Y quise entonces volver a ti,
a ese sitio donde el tiempo
aún no ha parido a la memoria,
para en ti reencontrarme,
para esconderme de nuevo
por siempre y hacerme
como al comienzo en tierra fértil,
un feto sembrado en tu vientre.

In your last four hours
of life
everything became a womb
while you escaped, nestled in light,
sheltered in your father's music.

And when, in that know-it-all machine,
the zeros won
I closed your eyes
and cried with the urgent tears
of the first time
when, lost and cast out
into the world I sought to look into your eyes.

And then I wanted to return to you,
to that place where time
has not yet given birth to memory,
to find myself again in you,
to hide myself again
forever and become
like at the start, in fertile ground,
a seed planted in your belly.

Trastiempo

A la memoria de Eugenio Montejo

Ayer caminaré por la noche
que terminó sobre esta línea.
Me detendré cuando sentí
que no fue un abismo
sino un puente colgante
sobre puntos suspensivos.
Hacia atrás avanzaré
persiguiendo una sombra,
tal vez la que seré, la que fue mía.
Al iniciarse la oscuridad
arribaré al momento
que entreveré antes.
En lo alto del crepúsculo
bajaré hasta la cima
de este poema que comenzaré
sobre esta línea, poco antes de partir.

Behindtime

In memory of Eugenio Montejo

Yesterday I'll walk through the night
that ended on this line.
I'll pause when I felt
that it wasn't a chasm
but a suspension bridge
hanging off periods.
I'll advance backwards
following a shadow,
maybe the one I'll be, the one that was mine.
When the darkness starts
I'll arrive at the moment
I will glimpse before.
At the height of sundown
I'll descend toward the summit
of this poem that I'll begin
on this line, just before I depart.

Un grito

Voy a zurcir
cada cosa
desde el comienzo:

El cuervo cae
junto a mi cuerpo

Grazna sobre la grama

Alguien me grita
sin puentes ni apuntes

El grito viene hacia mí

De lejos ve mi reloj

En picada bate sus alas

Su pico solo apunta
me apunta

Se clava como un clavo
en la tierra

Se entierra a mi lado

Desalado, nunca más

Sus ojos me miran
con el pico enterrado

A Scream

I'm going to mend
everything
from the beginning:

The raven lands
beside my body.

It caws on the grass

Someone screams at me
with neither bridges nor a script

The scream comes toward me

From far off it sees my watch

Plummeting it flaps its wings

Its beak only aims
it aims at me

It's nailed like a nail
in the earth

It's buried by my side

Wings clipped nevermore

Its eyes watch me
over the buried beak

Yo no sé quién despierta
Yo no sé

Oigo un grito
un grito que viene hacia mí

I don't know who wakes up
I don't know

I hear a scream
a scream coming toward me

Meditación sobre el porvenir

Me alcanzaron los años
y nunca supe cuándo.

De qué venir a contar ahora
que el temor dicta mi trato con las palabras.

Ahora, que apenas acierto a vislumbrar la virtud de los abismos.

Me alcanzaron como antes lo hicieran
con la hermana que no tuve
o que vino y se fue
o que no pudo.

Me alcanzaron impunes, vanidosos, cejijuntos.

Yo los reconozco por sus miradas arrogantes,
hijas del disimulo, engañadas de sí,
pues por cierto esconden un miedo riguroso
heredero de las pupilas de los moribundos.

Tantos años fueron precisos
y no supe cuándo.

Tanto trámite sin destino
para llegar aquí.

Meditation on the Future

The years caught up to me
and I never knew when.

What am I supposed to say now
that fear dictates my dealings with words.

Now that I can barely manage to make out the virtue of
abysses.

They caught up to me like they would have caught up
to the sister who I didn't have
or who came and went
or who couldn't.

They caught up to me unpunished, smug and unibrowed.

I recognize them by their arrogant glares,
daughters of disguise, self-deceived,
since by the way they hide an acute sense of fear
heir to the pupils of the dying.

So many years had to pass
and I didn't know when.

So much wasted effort
to get here.

Cartas del más allá

He escrito cartas a los muertos,
más por descuido
que ánimo de redimirlos
de sus fatales penurias.

Para mi sorpresa,
me han respondido
cordialmente.

Algunos acudiendo a un estricto silencio.
Otros, los más entusiastas,
refrendando sus mejores augurios
por nuestro próximo encuentro.

Letters from Beyond

I have written letters to the dead,
more out of carelessness
than any intent to relieve them
of their fatal hardships.

To my surprise,
they have responded
politely.

Some resorting to a strict silence.
Others, the most enthusiastic,
sending along their best wishes
until we meet again.

La visita

Yo había entrado sin percatarme, de pronto, sin entrar. No podría hablarse de un territorio, digamos, a la medida, era más bien ancho en las solapas. De cerca lucía desafortunado. Hablo de lo que uno presiente sin asomarse, de aquello que sucede en el camino de ascenso a las azoteas. Al llegar supe que algún trecho restaba. Habré de explicarme de otro modo: ya era el mismo que soy, alguien entre el punto B y el punto A (un sueño distendido, equidistante, a pocos pasos de la razón). Sí, estaba donde estuve desde siempre, allí quietecito, allá adentro, allí donde ya casi, donde casi, donde ya. Había entrado y tarde lo supe. Había llegado a mi antiguo rincón.

The Visit

I had entered without realizing it, suddenly, without entering. It was by no means a territory that was, shall we say, tailor-made, it was rather a bit wide in the lapels. At close range it showed off its misfortune. I'm talking about what one senses without leaning out to check, what takes place on the upward path toward the rooftops. When I arrived, I knew there was still a stretch left. I'll have to explain differently: I was already the same as I am, someone between Point B and Point A (a carefree dream, equidistant, a few steps away from reason). Yes, I was where I always was, there nice and still, there inside, there where almost there, where almost, where there. I had entered and I realized too late. I had arrived at my old spot.

Y al parecer sonríes

Yo te vi de niño en las noches
cuando mis mayores salían
a abrevar sus miedos al cementerio.

Yo te vi tomando una leche oscura,
poco antes de amanecer.

Me dijeron: "no es nada, no es nada,
péinate y guárdate por dentro".

Tú estabas, tal vez,
donde estás ahora.
Sabemos que nada ha ocurrido de allá para acá.

La leche sigue agria
y al parecer sonríes.

Dicen que pronto volverás,
que el cielo, a poco, va a esclarecer.

And You Seem to Smile

I saw you as a boy at night
when the grown-ups went out
to water their fears at the graveyard.

I saw you drinking dark milk,
just before dawn.

They told me: "it's nothing, it's nothing,
comb your hair and keep yourself inside."

You were, perhaps,
where you are now.
We know nothing has happened between there and here.

The milk's still sour
and you seem to smile.

They say you'll be back soon,
and the sky, bit by bit, will start to clear.

Un balcón

Pausadamente, las sombras
al esparcirse desalojan la luz
como a palabras que van quedando
huérfanas sobre algún verso.

Lo escrito se oscurece.

"Hubo un balcón donde un niño
se imaginaba las tardes, antes de su arribo"

¿Qué queda de ese lugar?
¿Solo el forcejeo entre el recuerdo y la oscurana?

¿Qué lumbre arropa ahora a ese niño?

Apenas se insinúa el ocaso
y ya hay una página difícil de leer.

¿Quién lo intenta?
¿Nosotros o aquél que nos busca en ella?

A Balcony

Deliberately, the shadows
displace the light as they spread
like words orphaned
on some line of poetry.

What's written grows dark.

"There was a balcony where a boy
imagined afternoons, before they arrived."

What remains of that place?
Only the clash between memory and darkness?

What warmth now wraps around that boy?

There is hardly a hint of sunset
and already the page is hard to read.

Who will try?
Will we, or will the one who seeks us on that page?

Enigma

Hay un silbo sin pájaro,
un canto para las aves ausentes,
un minuto olvidado que reclama su hora:
suma fortuita de sortilegios
embocados en algún nacimiento.

Hay un tedio enclavado en la insistencia:
una corona de espinas,
un enjambre sin verbos.

Pues de nada se vale la nada
para infligir penitencias.
Sus razones apenas nos rozan,
secretas como acertijos escondidos
en el habla misteriosa de las piedras.

Enigma

There's a chirp with no source,
a song for the absent birds,
a forgotten moment demanding its time:
accidental sum of spells
crammed into some birth.

There is a tedium embedded in persistence:
a crown of thorns,
a swarm without verbs.

Well, nothingness avails itself of nothing
for inflicting penance.
Its reasons hardly brush against us,
secret like hidden riddles
in the mysterious speech of the stones.

Saberes

...*Y los pájaros*

De nuevo los escucho
como quien sabe
que hay algo ya perdido
      para siempre

Por eso, algunas mañanas, me digo
al caminar, queriendo pensar que me comprendes:

¿y si hubo un instante que no ha sido,
qué propiciará el encuentro?

¿cómo tejer vínculos en el aire
cuando el aire nos sostiene?

Tal vez
eso
intentaron decirme
y no lo supe
      cantando partieron en vuelo.

Knowledge

...And the birds

I listen to them again
like one who knows
that something is already lost
       forever

That's why, some mornings, I tell myself
while walking, wanting to think you understand me:

if there was a moment that hasn't been,
what will bring about the encounter?

how does one weave bonds in the air
when the air holds us up?

Maybe
that
is what they tried to tell me
and I didn't realize
       they took flight singing.

Epitafio

Hubo homínidos y garrapatas,
pulmones altivos habituados a respirar.
Mientras fue
también eran los pájaros
                           y cantaban.
Eran
    frondosas
        las sombras,
    las mareas
        visitas esperadas.

Entre hendijas
    partía
        la luz mortecina de la tarde.

Era la luz
    y anochecía.

Epitaph

There were hominids and ticks,
haughty lungs accustomed to breathing.
While it was
the birds also were
                    and they were singing.

Dense
        were
                the shadows,
        the tides
                anticipated visits.

Between the cracks
        the dying
                light of afternoon was slipping away.

It was the light
        and night was falling.

Una historia verdadera

No te engañes.
Si hubo un tiempo en que todo parecía mentira,
tal vez fue así.

Pero fue allí
(y has de agradecerlo)
donde aprendiste a creer sin reparos.

Es cierto, hoy no sabes nada
con exactitud,
salvo que de uno a otro
amanecer suceden cosas.

Hay quienes piensan que los pájaros
se refugian en el canto
porque no quieren mentir.

Pero hay bandadas que buscan el sur
y se equivocan
creyendo, de veras,
que mañana se hará más tibio el sol.

A True Story

Don't deceive yourself.
If there was a time when everything seemed to be a lie,
maybe it was.

But it was there
(and you must be thankful for it)
where you learned to believe with no qualms.

It's true, today you know nothing
for certain,
except that from one dawn to the next
things happen.

There are those who think that birds
take shelter in song
because they don't want to lie.

But there are flocks that search for the south
and go the wrong way
believing sincerely
that tomorrow the sun will get warmer.

La Edad de Oro

Los domingos llegaban
cargados de noticias
escritas sin papel.

Desde muy temprano
nos adueñábamos
de una cómoda postura
para leer los rumores
que se urdían en el aire.

No escaseaban, por fortuna,
los buenos pregoneros, siempre
hábiles en la rendición de obstáculos.

En aquellos tiempos
las disidencias se dirimían
sin forzar precauciones:
se hablaba sin hablar.

Éramos un pueblo analfabeto
que un día
como cosa inofensiva
inventó la escritura.

Cuentan que existía la memoria
y en todo hombre aguardaba un mito.

The Golden Age

On Sundays they'd arrive
weighed down with news
written without paper.

From very early on
we'd take control of ourselves
in a comfortable position
to read the rumors
concocted in the air.

Luckily, we were never short
of good criers, always
skilled at conquering obstacles.

In those days
disagreements dissolved
with no forced precautions:
we spoke without speaking.

We were an illiterate people
that one day,
as if it were harmless,
invented writing.

They say memory existed
and every man contained a myth.

Los demorados

Los demorados llegaron.

Nadie los acechaba
una vez iniciado el nuevo milenio.

Entre matorrales apostaron
sus carpas y volvieron a la espera.

Desde su arribo, pocas noticias hemos tenido de ellos.

Se sabe que practican la prudencia
pero sería infamia propagar leyes
que quisieran omitir su peregrinar por la Tierra.

Atribuirles toda suerte de bondades
es una tentación que gestionan los adelantados.

Bastante tiempo hace que éstos se asomaron
a las ruinas del porvenir
y ahora sólo le temen a la extinción de los cangrejos.

Los demorados, un día, partieron sin avisar.

Ni rastros ni vestigios anunciaron su destino.

Desde entonces,
una lluvia pertinaz ha acrecentado los matorrales.

Consternada, la secta de los adelantados
ha decidido erigir el Nuevo Templo
(sobre el sitio donde los rumores dicen
que levantaron sus carpas).

The Delayed

The delayed arrived.

No one lay in wait for them
once the new millennium began.

In thickets they set up
their tents and went back to waiting.

Since their arrival, we've had little news of them.

It's known that they practice good judgment
but it would disgraceful to propagate laws
designed to leave out their pilgrimage over the Earth.

Attributing all sorts of goodness to them
is a common temptation administered by the advanced.

It's been awhile since they peeked out
at the ruins of the future
and now they fear only the extinction of crabs.

The delayed, one day, departed without warning.

No tracks or remains will announce their fate.

Since then,
a persistent rain has made the thickets grow.

Concerned, the sect of the advanced
has decided to erect the New Temple
(over the site where the rumors say
they raised their tents).

Sin detenerse, predican día y noche su inminente regreso.

Nosotros, con paciencia, los seguimos a la espera.

Without pause they preach, day and night, their imminent
                                                    return.

Patiently, we continue to wait.

NOTES ON THE WINTER

ANOTACIONES DE INVIERNO

Reverón, Macuto-New York (MoMA 2007)[1]

A Pedro Lastra y Eugenio Montejo,
en celebración de aquellos instantes preservados.

Qué queda allí donde viviste, qué queda de tu Castillete.
Ahora aquí, en esta ciudad, el blanco de tus lienzos
no sólo oculta el color de nuestros trópicos,
el sonido incesante de sus bosques de palmeras.

Ahora es la luz de una foto velada,
aquélla en que estuvimos y ya no,
borrados por una avalancha de lodo y muerte.

Aquélla que escondía el rumor de la montaña,
el recuerdo de una tarde ya perdida, ya lejana,
una tarde como ésta, fría, ajena, cubierta de otro blanco,
cubierta, como esta ciudad, por un manto de nieve.

Reverón, Macuto-New York (MoMA 2007)[1]

To Pedro Lastra and Eugenio Montejo,
in celebration of those preserved moments.

What's left of where you lived, what's left of your Castillete.
Here, now, in this city, the white of your canvas
hides not just the color of our tropics,
the incessant sound of their palm tree forests.

Now it's the light of an overexposed photo,
the one in which we once were but no longer,
erased by an avalanche of mud and death.

The one that concealed the murmurs of the mountain,
the memory of an afternoon now lost, now distant,
an afternoon like this one, cold and foreign, covered in
                                              another white,
covered, like this city, in a blanket of snow.

Cuento de hadas

De nuevo la mañana
y hoy
una niña muerta,
una niña de ocho años
—acotan las noticias—
y su perro.
Ambos aplastados
por una rama cubierta de hielo.
Yo hubiera preferido decir de cristal
y hablar de la magia de los cuentos de hadas.
No de las trampas que disimula el invierno.
Desearía detenerme en el resplandor
de estas insólitas ramas,
imaginar estalactitas
suspendidas
en las barbas de los árboles
o en el atareado sueño
de una savia ya vieja y adormecida.
Yo hubiera querido celebrar
la fortuna
de mi extranjera mirada.
Sentarme a la ventana y escuchar
y tan sólo escuchar
el difícil idioma de la nieve que cae.
Yo aspiraba a comprender su blancura,
la de una lengua que hacía serena
y de pronto se reveló
en un crujir inesperado,
en un estallido de vidrios.

Una niña y su perro
han muerto.

Fairy Tale

Morning again
and today
a dead girl,
an eight-year-old girl
—specifies the news—
and her dog.
Both crushed
by a branch covered in ice.
I would have preferred to say in crystal
and to speak of the magic of fairy tales.
Not of the traps laid by the winter.
I'd wish to pause on the shining
of those unusual branches,
to imagine stalactites
suspended
from the beards of the trees
or from the hectic dreams
of old and sleepy sap.
I would have liked to celebrate
the good fortune
of my foreign gaze.
To sit by the window and listen
and only listen
to the difficult language of the falling snow.
Hoping to understand its whiteness,
that of a language that seems serene
then suddenly reveals itself
with an unexpected crack,
with a shattering of glass.

A girl and her dog
have died.

Yo hubiera querido,
Yo hubiera deseado hablar de otra cosa.

I would have liked,
I would have wished to talk about something else.

La punta de un lápiz

> Every day, every night of our lives, we're leaving little bits of
> ourselves, flakes of this and that, behind. Where do they go,
> these bits and pieces of ourselves?
>
> RAYMOND CARVER

Es fácil consolidar la vista
en la punta de un lápiz,
pretender el mundo en ella.

La mirada se despliega, persigue
los pasos de un destino ajeno.

El hombre barre el polvo
que se ha ido acumulando durante meses.

No es invierno aún, pero no importa
—hay vidas donde siempre las pisadas dejan huellas en la nieve,
aunque no haya nieve—.

Barre los despojos de los días
—de lo que ha sido su cuerpo—.
Arrincona en las esquinas los malos pensamientos.

Enciende la televisión:

"Es cierto, no nos conocemos.
Te he visto poco, tan solo de reojo en los espejos.
No sé qué decirte.

The Point of a Pencil

Every day, every night of our lives, we're leaving little bits of
ourselves, flakes of this and that, behind. Where do they go,
these bits and pieces of ourselves?

RAYMOND CARVER

It's easy to consolidate one's sight
on the point of a pencil,
to seek the world in it.

The gaze unfolds, it pursues
the footsteps of someone else's fate.

The man sweeps up the dust
that has been building up for months.

It's not yet winter, but that doesn't matter
—there are lives where footsteps always leave prints in the snow,
even when there is no snow.

He sweeps up the waste of the days
—of what has been his body.
He piles all the bad thoughts into corners.

He turns on the television:

"It's true, we don't know each other.
I haven't seen you often, just out of the corner of my eye, in mirrors.
I don't know what to tell you.

He hecho muchas cosas. Comer, beber, dormir.
Inevitablemente he dormido.
Quizás es lo único que he hecho".

La apaga.

Barre sin pericia, pero barre,
junta pelusas, recuerdos, cabellos.

El hombre, sin saberlo, avanza.

Camina sobre un campo minado,
sobre los restos de su propio cuerpo.

Todo es tan incierto. Te ves, te tocas, te hueles:
por un momento piensas que vives en él.

No seas tonto, no seas tonto —te insisten.

Una calle me basta, un paisaje acotado por dos esquinas.

Vivo en un piso impar,
cuando me asomo
por mi única ventana
me observo en los demás
y me digo:

"Somos una cosa que anda y piensa
y se dice
y desdice
y te dice
y nos dice.
Que habla y enmudece.
Que se repite y miente.
Una cosa tartamuda.

I've done many things. Eat, drink, sleep.
Inevitably I've slept.
Maybe that's the only thing I've done."

He turns it off.

He sweeps without skill, but he sweeps,
he picks up lint, memories, hairs.

The man, without knowing it, advances.

He walks over a minefield,
over the remains of his own body.

Everything is so uncertain. You see yourself, you touch
yourself, you smell yourself:
for a moment you think you live in him.

Don't be silly, don't be silly, they insist.

One street is enough for me, one landscape enclosed between
two corners.

I live on an odd floor,
when I lean out
my only window
I see myself in others
and I say to myself:

"We are something that walks and thinks
and tells itself
and retracts
and tells you
and tells us.
That talks and falls silent.

Colesterol malo,
genoma,
aura,
venáticos humores.
Una tontería quizás,
sin suma,
sin fin".

Enciendo la radio.

Dicen que la guerra es buena:
es cuestión de reconsiderar la higiene.

La gente muere por la patria,
por la honra que jamás claudica.

Se exoneran las deudas.

En mi país mueren también,
cada treinta minutos lo hacen de frente o de espalda.
No importa. Siempre una bala los atraviesa.

Apago la radio.

Anoche pensé que iba a morir,
pero pensé, sobre todo,
que antes de que lo supieras
se enterarían las ardillas.

He mudado la mesa hasta la ventana,
desde allí la sombra de los árboles
se emparenta con la de mi lápiz.

That repeats itself and lies.
A stuttering thing.
Bad cholesterol,
genome,
aura,
moonstruck humors.
A load of nonsense perhaps,
without sum,
without end."

I turn on the radio.

They say war is good:
it's a question of reconsidering hygiene.

People die for their homeland,
for the honor that never gives in.

The debts are waived.

They die in my country too,
they do it every thirty minutes facing forward or backward.
It doesn't matter. A bullet always passes through them.

I turn off the radio.

Last night I thought I was going to die,
but I thought, above all,
that before you knew about it
the squirrels would find out.

I've moved the table over to the window,
from there the shadow of the trees
marries into the shadow of my pencil.

Hay una sombra común a la madera.

Ahora puedo emprender
la tarea de escribir de día sobre las sombras.

Si la vecina supiera todo esto
dejaría de saludarme.

Nunca es confiable la gente que se refugia
en la oscuridad a pleno sol.

Es sabido que el polvo se acumula por la desidia:
la dejadez de una inerte existencia.
Sin adecuados regímenes sanitarios
toda civilización peligra, se hace polvo, desaparece.

Abro la bandeja de mi correo electrónico.
Las noticias hablan del clima en otros países,
de los glaciares descongelados y la tibieza de los cadáveres que
yacían en ellos,
del recalentamiento mundial, y los vientos de guerra,
de la hambruna africana y las adopciones hollywoodenses,
de un venadito perdido en los suburbios de Pennsylvania,
del fanático que atrapó un jonrón en el estadio,
de los miles de muertos del último tsunami,
de la vuelta al siglo XIX en mi país.

Al barrer, las ventanas deben permanecer cerradas,
se debe evitar la agresión de aires intrusos.
Como no se trata de separar
distintos géneros de despojos,
se pueden acumular en un solo montón
pelos, pestañas caídas y gotas de sudor
junto a los vestigios de otros cuerpos
que también hacen su vida en este vecindario.

There is a shadow common to wood.

Now I can undertake
the task of writing by day on the shadows.

If the neighbor knew all this
she wouldn't say hello anymore.

One can never trust people who take shelter
in darkness while the sun shines.

It is well known that dust builds up due to apathy:
the negligence of an inert existence.
Without adequate health systems
every civilization endangers, turns to dust, disappears.

I open my email inbox.
The news tells of the climate in other countries,
melted glaciers and the warmth of the cadavers that lay
                                              within them,
global rewarming, and the winds of war,
famine in Africa and adoptions in Hollywood,
a fawn lost in the suburbs of Pennsylvania,
a fan who caught a home run in the stadium,
the thousands dead in the latest tsunami,
my country's return to the nineteenth century.

While sweeping, the windows must remain closed,
one must avoid the aggression of intruding airs.
It is not a question of separating
distinct genres of waste,
one may pile in a single mound
hairs, fallen eyelashes and drops of sweat
along with the vestiges of other bodies
that also make their living in this neighborhood.

De este modo, si a ver vamos,
un montoncito reunido así
se parece mucho a una pequeña junta de condominio
donde se agrupan para compartir reclamos
las cotidianas víctimas de nuestra comunidad.

La escritura no es caso aparte,
en ella también la punta del lápiz se pulveriza,
se convierte en trazo sobre la página,
apenas el efímero testimonio de una vaga intimidad.

Convertida en huella precaria,
sigue los pasos de un hombre
sobre la nieve, aunque no haya nieve,
esa que en enero,
de nuevo,
cubrirá extensos
y anónimos cementerios.

In this way, if we mean to see,
a small mound piled up this way
looks a lot like a little tenant meeting
where the everyday victims of our community
come together to share complaints.

Writing is not a case apart,
it also pulverizes the point of the pencil,
turning it into a line on the page,
the fleeting testament to some vague intimacy.

Turned into a precarious print,
it follows the footsteps of a man
on the snow, even when there is no snow,
the snow that in January,
once again,
will cover vast
and nameless graveyards.

POSTCARDS FROM THE MIDWEST

POSTALES DEL MIDWEST

Canción para Phillip, mi estudiante de español

Phillip asiste a clases
diariamente
con su verde uniforme.

Phillip es casi un niño
que confunde
México con Madrid.

A Phillip le gusta
que le cuenten
historias de ultramar.

Que le hablen de las victorias
de Lucius Quinctius Cincinnatus
y su legado en Gettysburg.

Phillip conoce sólo tres cosas:
la obediencia a la patria,
al dinero
y a Dios.

En esa cárcel ha vivido siempre
sin maldad.

Phillip pronto
se irá a la guerra
como Mambrú.

¿Qué lengua olvidada
traerá de Babel?

Song for Phillip, My Student in Spanish Class

Phillip comes to class
every day
in his green uniform.

Phillip is almost a child
who mixes up
Mexico and Madrid.

Phillips likes it
when they tell him
stories from overseas.

When they speak of the victories
of Lucius Quinctius Cincinnatus
and his legacy at Gettysburg.

Phillip knows only three things:
obedience to country,
to money,
and to God.

He has always lived in that jail cell
without malice.

Soon, Phillip
will go marching in
like the saints.

What forgotten language
will he bring back from Babel?

¿En qué tiempo aprenderá
a conjugar
matar?

¿Quién ocupará su pupitre
y seguirá sus lecciones
cuando no esté?

In what tense will he learn
to conjugate
matar?

Who will move into his desk
and carry on his lessons
when he's gone?

Almorzando en un Burger King

Escribir un poema en una servilleta
—como éste que ahora escribo—
sentado en una mesa blanca y rosada
—como ésta en que estoy sentado—
comiendo una hamburguesa "Big King"
con papas fritas y coca-cola
—como la que como, mientras hago
una pausa en lo que escribo—
no puede terminar de otra manera
que con la frase final del ticket
que está sobre mi bandeja:
"Have a nice day <smile>"
—como la sonrisa de la cajera,
la instantánea y única musa de este poema—.

Lunch at Burger King

Writing a poem on a napkin
—like the one I'm writing now—
sitting at a pink and white table
—like the one I'm sitting at now—
eating a Big King burger
with fries and a Coke
—like the one I'm eating, as I take
a break in which to write—
couldn't end with anything
except the final line of the receipt
that's on my tray:
"Have a nice day :)"
—like the smile of the cashier,
the instantaneous, unique muse of this poem.

La voz de la Divinidad

"Oh God, Oh my God".

Estas voces ajenas
me hablan
desnudas
en su hirsuta lengua.
Arriba o debajo,
no lo sé.

Convocan a un Dios
con gozosos monosílabos,
con prolongados gemidos;
sin apurar su llegada,
sin desjuntarse.

Yo, sin ser el de la Cruz,
la reconozco.

Tal es la voz de la Divinidad,
cuando extraña se ayunta
—Amado con amada, tan alto, tan alto—
en este idioma de ardientes bramidos.

The Voice of Divinity

"Oh my God, oh my God."

These unseen voices
speak to me
naked
in their bristly language.
Above or below,
I don't know.

They call out to a God
with pleasured monosyllables,
with lengthy moans;
without rushing his arrival,
without coming apart.

Although I'm not de la Cruz,
I recognize it.

Such is the voice of Divinity
when it strangely yokes together
—Lover with beloved, so high, so high—
in this language of ardent cries.

Nocturno de Oklahoma

A Marcelo Rioseco

Alguien tocó la puerta
en la madrugada
y al abrir
entró un tornado
arrasando con todo;
lo siguió un caballo desbocado
que para apaciguarse
buscó escondite en un armario.

Los vecinos siguieron dormidos.

Todo me resultó extraño
pues antes de que Eolo encabritado
se llevara hasta el televisor
no hubo anuncios de peligro
en los reportes del tiempo.

Este mensaje lo escribo ahora
                    desde el aire
y lo dejo en el viento
                    con la esperanza
de que pasado
                    el torbellino,
la brisa lo arrime
                    a buen puerto
y no a las manos
                    de otro náufrago
        sin botellas
recorriendo las playas
                    de una isla incierta
fabulada en bestiarios
                    y catálogos de tifones.

Oklahoma Nocturne

To Marcelo Rioseco

Someone knocked on the door
at the crack of dawn
and when it opened
in came a tornado,
leveling everything;
following it was a runaway horse
trying to calm itself down
by hiding away in the closet.

The neighbors stayed asleep.

It all seemed strange to me,
since before this riled-up Aeolus
swept away everything
including the TV
there was no word of danger
in the weather reports.

I now write this message
                    from the air
and I leave it on the wind
                    with the hope
that once the cyclone
                    has passed
the breeze will lead it
                    to a good harbor
and not to the hands
                    of another castaway
          without a bottle
pacing the beaches
                    of an uncertain island
invented in bestiaries
                    and lists of typhoons.

MEN AT WORK

OBREROS EN LA VÍA

Renuncien a defender las buenas costumbres[11]

Ustedes son los que tienen miedo de morir.
Nosotros no.
Somos hombres bombas.

Estamos en el centro de lo insoluble.

Ustedes, entre el bien y el mal,
se detienen en la única frontera.

Su muerte es un drama cristiano
en una cama, un cáncer, un ataque al corazón.
La nuestra, la comida diaria, la fosa común.

Somos una empresa moderna, rica.
Ustedes, el estado quebrado, una zafra de incompetentes.

Tenemos métodos ágiles de gestión.
Ustedes son lentos, burocráticos.

Luchamos en terreno propio.
Ustedes, en tierra extraña
muriendo de miedo, cada hora.

Estamos bien armados, al ataque.
A ustedes los persigue la manía del humanismo.
Somos crueles, no conversamos con la piedad.

Ustedes nos han transformado en "super stars" del crimen.
Los tenemos de payasos.

Refuse to Defend Good Manners[II]

You're the ones who are afraid of dying.
Not us.
We are human bombs.

We're at the center of the insoluble.

You all, between good and bad,
wait around at the only border.

Your death is a Christian drama
in a bed, a cancer, a heart attack.
Ours is the daily meal, the mass grave.

We are a modern, wealthy business.
You all, the failed state, a crop of incompetents.

We have agile management methods.
You are slow, bureaucratic.

We fight on home ground.
You, on foreign soil
dying of fear by the minute.

We are well armed to attack.
You're hounded by the mania of humanism.
We are cruel, we don't converse with pity.

You have transformed us into "superstars" of crime.
We see you as clowns.

Nos llaman "los barones del polvo",
y por miedo o por amor nos ayudan en el barrio.
A ustedes los odian.

Nuestras armas y mercancías vienen de afuera,
somos "globales".
Ustedes, nuestros clientes.

¿Solución? No hay solución, hermano.

Somos el inicio de algo tardío.

Somos hormigas devoradoras,
escondidas en los rincones.

Renuncien a defender las buenas costumbres.

Estamos todos en el centro de lo insoluble.

Como dijo el divino Dante:
"Pierdan las esperanzas, estamos en el infierno".

They call us "the powder barons"
and out of fear or love they help us in the barrio.
They hate you.

Our wares and weapons come from the outside,
we are "global."
You are our clients.

Solution? There is no solution, brother.

We're the start of something that came late.

We are ravenous ants,
hiding in the corners.

Refuse to defend good manners.

We are all at the center of the insoluble.

As the divine Dante said:
"Abandon hope, we are in hell."

Amanecer en el Paseo de la Reforma

Antes de que salga el sol
la vida está inquieta,
soñamos despertar pero no lo hacemos.

No es tiempo de cultivo.
Tláloc, ansioso de ofrendas, permanece.
Y a lo lejos oímos tambores
como si anunciaran la guerra florida.

Son las 6:30 en el Paseo de la Reforma:
los pochtecas salen con sus vasos humeantes
de los Starbucks de las vidriosas torres financieras;
los indigentes siguen durmiendo a los costados
de las vidriosas torres financieras;
hay tamales y transeúntes en las esquinas;
oficiales con chamarras fosforescentes
contradicen los semáforos;
hombres de negro, encapuchados,
con relucientes metralletas, resguardan la calma;
gente en indumentaria contra el colesterol
trota con chihuahuas atados a sus pasos;
obreros con rostros campesinos
emergen en masa de los subterráneos
mientras otros, mejor ataviados, ruedan
en dirección contraria en bicicletas de alquiler;
huelguistas de hambre salen de sus carpas, mugrientos,
frente al Instituto de Salubridad e Higiene.

Entretanto, los guerreros águilas ostentan
sus coloridos y emplumados escudos
y cantan en coro:

Dawn on Paseo de la Reforma

Before the sun comes up
life is restless,
we dream of waking but we don't.

It's not planting time.
Tlaloc, anxious for offerings, remains.
And in the distance we hear drums
as if declaring flower war.

It's 6:30 on Paseo de la Reforma;
the pochtecas emerge with steaming cups
from the Starbucks of the glass financial towers;
the indigent carry on sleeping beside
the glass financial towers;
there are tamales and pedestrians on the corners;
police wearing fluorescent coats
contradict the traffic lights;
men in black, masked,
with shiny automatic guns, keep the peace;
runners rebelling against cholesterol
trot by with chihuahuas tied to their steps;
workers with campesino faces
emerge en masse from the underground
while others, better dressed, roll
the opposite direction on rented bikes;
hunger strikers come out of their tents, filthy,
in front of the Institute of Health and Hygiene.

Meanwhile, the eagle warriors show off
their colorful plumed shields
and sing in chorus:

"Aquí nadie teme la muerte en la guerra
esta es nuestra gloria
este tu mandato
¡Oh, dador de la vida!"

Así, "orgullosa de sí misma", en duermevela:
"se levanta la ciudad de México-Tenochtitlán".

"No one here fears death in war
this is our glory
this your command
Oh, giver of life!"

And so, "proud of itself," shaking off sleep:
"the city of México-Tenochtitlán arises."

Los secretos vicios de Tenochtitlán

El inframundo no sólo es fuego
ni los hornos de Vulcano.
Allá hay otras formas de lidiar
con los trasuntos de la vida,
desde muy abajo.
No es un lugar donde laboran solos
los carboneros que le proveen humo
a la boca del Popocatépetl.
También hay seres acuosos y asalariados,
buzos de aguas negras que trashuman sumergidos
16 kilómetros de drenajes, debajo de las alcantarillas.
Gente avezada en la faena
de enfrentar a solas la oscuridad,
entre estiércol, desechos y cadáveres.
Gente acostumbrada a destapar los secretos vicios
y entuertos de los que viven arriba.

The Secret Vices of Tenochtitlán

The underworld is not just fire
and Vulcan's ovens.
It offers other ways to cope
with the mirror images of life
from far below.
It's not a place where only coalmen work
providing smoke
for the mouth of Popocatépetl.
There are also watery, wage-earning beings,
divers in muck who migrate submerged
through 16 kilometers of sewers, below the drains.
People adept at the task
of facing the darkness alone,
among excrement, rubbish and cadavers.
People accustomed to uncovering the secret vices
and wrongs of those who live above.

Universidad-Indios Verdes

¿Para qué forzar los sueños y las pesadillas
si aquí todo convulsiona hasta domesticar el asombro?
Esto, solo en parte, lo supo Breton con sus ojos ingenuos,
al pasearlos por las superficies de estas tierras.

Para entonces los subsuelos eran profundidades ganadas
por el agua, el lodo y ruinas anteriores
a los dioses de Lautréamont.

Desde hace medio siglo, sin apelar a la imaginación,
los habitantes de este valle transitan
por debajo de las calles,
excavando, día a día, el sustento.

Un mercado abigarrado y florido
(de ofertas y padecimientos)
viaja entre túneles y vagones
apretujando la existencia de los que van de prisa,
de los que buscan atajos debajo de todo.

Un ciego que tal vez no mira, toca una melodía
en un piano eléctrico con la diestra,
al tiempo que siniestramente lleva el ritmo,
entre tropezones, con un vaso que es maraca y alcancía;
chocolates de calidad y cacahuates se anuncian
a 10 pesos ("a lo que valen y a lo que cuestan");
mujeres con tapabocas miran de reojo a parejas que se abrazan
y besan como topos en tiempos de cópula.

Universidad-Indios Verdes

Why force out dreams and nightmares
if everything here convulses until it tames amazement?
This, only in part, is what Breton realized with his naïve eyes
as they drifted across the surface of these lands.

In those days the subsoil was a depth conquered
by water, mud, and ruins more ancient
than the gods of Lautréamont.

Since half a century ago, without resorting to imagination,
the inhabitants of this valley have traveled
underneath the streets,
excavating, day by day, its foundations.

A bustling, flowery market
(with special offers and suffering)
travels along tunnels and train cars
squashing in the existence of those who rush by,
of those who seek shortcuts beneath it all.

A blind man, maybe not watching, plays a melody
on an electric piano with his right hand
as he keeps the beat sinister with the other,
between trip-ups, with a cup that is maraca and collection box;
quality chocolates and peanuts are advertised
for 10 pesos each ("they cost what they're worth");
women in face masks look sideways at couples that embrace
and kiss like moles in heat.

Toda especie de anunciantes entra y sale de los vagones,
estación tras estación: vendedores de libros de autoayuda
y biografías del Che; predicadores evangélicos;
pregoneros de chicles y paletas
para el bien de gargantas y bocas;
aturdidos sordomudos; parapléjicos enyesados;
dj`s enmochilados y cantantes con guitarras electroacústicas
que ofrecen baladas y rock, en inglés y en español.

Todos forcejean cuerpo a cuerpo
como lisiados de extintas batallas.

Nada de esto registró en su bitácora el padre del surrealismo,
ni mientras visitaba estos parajes
ni al macerar el inconsciente en las riberas del Sena.

Every kind of advertiser enters and exits the train cars,
station to station: people selling self-help books
and biographies of Che; evangelical preachers;
vendors of chewing gum and lozenges
for the good of throats and mouths;
dazed deaf-mutes; paraplegics in casts;
DJs with backpacks and singers with electric-acoustic guitars
who offer ballads and rock in English and Spanish.

All struggle, body against body,
like the wounded of extinct battles.

The father of surrealism noted none of this in his log,
not while visiting these stops
nor while marinating his subconscious in the waters of the Seine.

Los niños plateados

Los niños plateados
juegan con candela
para prolongar el rojo
de los semáforos.

Además de malabares
popocan *por la boca*
y hacen vírgulas que queman.

Así hablan ellos.

Sin necesidad de labrar testimonios
en piedras pintadas.

The Silver Children

The silver children
play with candles
to prolong the red
of the traffic lights.

Besides juggling
they *popocan* through their mouths
and exhale burning virgules.

That's how they talk.

With no need to carve testimony
on painted stones.

Reclusorio femenil de Santa Martha Acatitla

Y me pidieron
    cuando salga
    escriba un poema
    hable de nosotras
y me dijeron
imploraron
mandaron recados
    no nos olvide
    por si algún día
que afuera
    y niños tenemos
    chaparros
    y aún más pequeñitos
    a punto de nacer
y adentro
    pues nunca se sabe
que todo es injusto
que nada da igual
pero que les lea
que apacigua la rabia
que está bien
y así son
así son las historias
que les siga leyendo
o los cantos
y que algún día
ya veremos
y que gracias

Santa Martha Acatitla Women's Prison

And they asked me
    when you leave
    write a poem
    speak of us
and they told me
they begged
they sent messages
    don't forget us
    in case someday
on the outside
    and we have kids
    toddlers
    and even littler
    about to be born
and inside
    well, you never know
everything's unfair
it's not all the same
but read to us
the anger subsides
it's alright
and that's how they are
that's how the stories are
that I keep reading to them
or the songs
and some day
we'll see
and thank you

Zamuros

Con envidia de los coyotes,
volando, de la serranía,
sobre Tenochtitlán caía
muchedumbre de zopilotes

JOSÉ JUAN TABLADA

En mi país los zopilotes se llaman zamuros
y vuelan sobre mi ciudad, en bandadas circulares,
desde que amanece.

Dicen que lo hacen,
avizores de la basura y los cadáveres
que les brinda la ciudad.

He sabido que por acá,
guardando las distancias,
no son distintos los oficios de los zopilotes,
cuyas alas, sacrificadas en el Templo Mayor,
oscurecían el sol antes de que llegara el smog.

Ahora, en ambas latitudes,
escasean las águilas que aún cacen serpientes.

En estos tiempos, sobre todo, abundan las moscas.

Zamuros

Jealous of the coyotes,
flying, from the mountains,
there fell over Tenochtitlán
a horde of vultures.

JOSÉ JUAN TABLADA

In my country, zopilotes are called zamuros
and they fly over my city in circular flocks,
starting at dawn.

They say they do so,
watching over the garbage and cadavers
that the city provides them.

I've learned that here,
keeping their distance,
the same role is played by zopilotes,
whose wings, sacrificed at Templo Mayor,
darkened the sun before the coming of the smog.

Now, at both latitudes,
the eagles that still hunt snakes grow scarce.

These days, above all, there are flies.

En una estación del metro no vista por Pound
(en Caracas no en París)

> *The apparition of these faces in the crowd;*
> *Petals on a wet, black bough.*
>
> EZRA POUND

El hombre de escaso muñón
descendió a los infiernos,
serpenteó entre sombras inválidas
arrastrando sus muletas como un gimnasta.

De un brinco entre tantos
alcanzó la boca de un vagón.

Hablaba de sida y albúmina humana
a las soterradas multitudes.

Sus manos extendidas como reliquias
imploraban a un bosque de húmedos rostros,
pétalos purulentos sobre negras ramas.

In a Metro Station Not Seen by Pound
(in Caracas, not Paris)

> *The apparition of these faces in the crowd;*
> *Petals on a wet, black bough.*
>
> EZRA POUND

The man with a meager stump
descended into hell,
he slithered between invalid shadows
dragging his crutches like a gymnast.

With one hop out of many
he reached the mouth of a subway car.

He spoke of AIDS and human albumin
to the buried multitudes.

His hands, extended like relics,
begged in a forest of wet faces,
purulent petals on black boughs.

El extranjero

Ese hombre se visita a sí mismo
en las mañanas,
puntual;
odia las demoras.

Riñe consigo
en una lengua indescifrable.

Camina entre extraños
en callejones desiertos.

Algunos dirían que es un animal extraviado,
alguien que por voluntad
o accidente cedió su manada.

Alguien que come su comida a solas
y prefiere conversar con espejos.

Ese hombre no requiere divanes
y cuando escucha ruidos
en el sótano
no se asoma,
sabe que nada pasa.

Es un hombre sin medias tintas.
Se repite a sí mismo
cada mañana
y sale a cumplir sus deberes.

Sin dudas, un ciudadano común.

The Foreigner

That man visits himself
in the morning,
punctually;
he hates delays.

He quarrels with himself
in an indecipherable tongue.

He walks between strangers
through deserted alleyways.

Some might say he's a stray animal,
someone who willingly
or accidentally relinquished his pack.

Someone who eats his meals alone
and prefers to talk with mirrors.

That man has no need
to lie on couches
and when he hears noises
in the cellar
he doesn't look down,
he knows it's nothing.

He is a man without half measures.
He repeats himself
every morning
and leaves to fulfill his duties.

No doubts, an everyday citizen.

Ciudadanía

Todo hombre, tanto el mejor como el más miserable, lleva consigo un misterio que, de ser conocido, le haría odioso a todos los demás.

WALTER BENJAMIN

Ése escupe en las aceras
con el orgullo hinchado:

cerdo escapado de los mataderos.

Aquél voltea el rostro
ante el rostro miserable:

el que pide en cada esquina.

Éste apura el paso
para no dar una limosna:

para evitar el idioma de los deformes y mutilados.

Ésos, entre dientes, maldicen el olor de las alcantarillas.

Éstos, náufragos sin anclas, sobrevivientes de humedales.

Aquéllos, ni mártires, ni santos ni suicidas.

Ésos, éstos, aquéllos,
todos ellos
también soy yo.

Citizenship

*Every person, the best as well as the most wretched, carries around
a secret that would make him hateful to all others if it became known.*

WALTER BENJAMIN

That one spits on the sidewalk
with swollen pride:

swine escaped from the slaughterhouse.

The other turns his face
away from the wretched face:

the one that begs on every corner.

This one picks up his pace
so as not to give alms:

to avoid the language of the deformed and the mutilated.

Those ones, under their breath, curse at the smell of the sewers.

These ones, castaways without anchors, survivors from the
    wetlands.

The others, not martyrs, nor saints, nor suicides.

Those ones, these ones, the others,
all of them are also me.

Hábitos ciudadanos

Dos que no se han visto nunca
o tal vez sí (da lo mismo)
caminan uno junto al otro.
Se desconocen ciudadanamente,
defienden su derecho a la indiferencia.

Uno no piensa nada del otro
y viceversa.
Mantienen sus pasos juntos.
Juntos buscan su destino.

Si se vieron antes o será la última vez
da igual.

Todo se hará olvido
sin borraduras.

Todo se hará como el día anterior.

Civic Habits

Two who've never seen each other before
or maybe have (it doesn't matter)
walk, one beside the other.
They don't know each other civically,
they defend their right to indifference.

One thinks nothing of the other
and vice versa.
They keep pace together.
Together they seek their fate.

If they saw each other before or if this will be the last time
makes no difference.

Everything will be forgotten
with no eraser marks.

Everything will be like the day before.

Extracto del santoral del buen revolucionario

Cosa extraña,
hoy nuestro predicador
amaneció abúlico.
Sus enemigos, esas bestias
roñosas de hábitos insaciables,
no alcanzaron a distraer
la frugalidad de sus sueños.

Extract from the Book of Saints of the Good Revolutionary

How strange!
Today our preacher
woke up apathetic.
His enemies, those filthy
beasts with insatiable habits,
could do nothing to distract
the frugality of his dreams.

El miliciano

No se moleste
comandante,
ordéneme callar
hasta donde llegue el silencio.

Si para que reinara la luz
fue necesaria,
no más,
su llegada,
no han de ser balbuceos míos
los que requieran su enojo.

Profeso la inevitable lealtad
de la brizna ante el huracán.

Aquí nadie se equivoca.

La patria nos reclama,
sin reclamos.

Asintamos,
asentemos con nuestro silencio
(hasta donde nos llegue)
la máxima suma
de su felicidad.

The Militiaman

Don't be upset
comandante,
order me to shut my mouth
as far as silence goes.

If the only thing necessary
for light to reign
was simply
your arrival,
the babbling that required your anger
would not be mine.

I profess the inevitable loyalty
of a blade of grass in a hurricane.

Here, nobody makes mistakes.

The homeland makes demands of us,
no demands.

We shall consent.
We shall put down, along with our silence
(as far as it goes),
the maximum sum
of your happiness.

Dos patrias

¡Así es la gente!
Aprestan el oído,
rumorean,
se esconden detrás de los helechos.

Alguien pasa y dice
                    lo que dicen.

Levantan consignas,
agitan sus alas
                    de mal agüero.

Sólo son susurros,
cosas que no suceden.

Nadie sabe nada detrás de mi puerta.

Allá,
en el otro país,
lejos,
también se vive
                    dicen
                              entre la carcoma y las arengas.
Aquí, hay sólo susurros,
falsos temblores,
cosas que no escuchamos,
que no escuchamos,
que no suceden.

Dos patrias, dos patrias tengo yo:
¿O son una las dos?

Two Homelands

To Marina Gasparini

That's what people are like!
They prick up their ears,
they gossip,
they hide behind the ferns.

Someone passes and says
                    what they say.

They lift up slogans,
they flap their wings
                    birds of ill omen.

They're only whispers,
things that don't happen.

Nobody knows anything behind my door.

There,
in the other country,
far away,
there is also life,
                    they say
                            between woodworms and diatribes.
Here there are only whispers,
false tremors,
things that we don't hear,
that we don't hear,
that don't happen.

Two homelands, I have two homelands.
Or are the two one?

Memoria de una antigua amistad

Para aquellos afectos devenidos camaradas

Ya nos veremos de nuevo
en los lugares donde alguna vez
creímos que se haría infranqueable la amistad.

Después de todo esto,
cuando cesen los batallones
y se hayan recogido las cartas
nos descubriremos acodados sobre mesas sin trastos,
para vernos nuevamente
a la cara,
sin olvidar lo que creímos
—o por no olvidarlo—
pero sin borronear lo acontecido
desde aquel paréntesis hasta acá.

Y cuando llegue ese día,
lo sabemos, se nos hará difícil
encontrar las palabras comunes,
aquéllas que apartadas se refugiaron en libros
que ahora se nos antojan escritos
en extraños idiomas; aquéllas,
ahora degolladas en los desvencijados rieles de la Historia.

Entonces habremos de preguntarnos:

¿en qué calle ya no pudimos voltear?
¿en qué esquina dejó de ser por siempre la hermandad?

Memory of an Old Friendship

For those old friends turned comrades

We'll see each other again
in those places where we once
believed friendship would become insurmountable.

After all this,
when the battalions cease
and the playing cards have been collected
we will find ourselves leaning on empty tables,
to see ourselves freshly
face to face,
without forgetting what we believed
—or so as not to forget it—
but without scribbling down what took place
between that parenthesis and here.

And when that day arrives,
we know it will be hard for us
to find the common words,
those that hide away, isolated in books,
that now catch our eye
despite being written in strange languages; those
that now have their throats cut on the rickety rails of History.

Then we'll have to ask ourselves:

at which street could we no longer turn?
at which corner did brotherhood cease to exist?

Un país

Cuando el forastero llegó
ya todos se habían ido.

Cuentan que solo tuvo entre sus manos
acuarelas de niños que pintaban un país
donde la nieve era apenas un tacto imaginado.

Un lugar amañado por la astucia
y las costumbres de la luz,
que incauta resguardaba escondrijos
para que las sombras perpetuaran traiciones,
desde antes de nacer.

Cuentan sus ingenuos dibujos
(ahora devorados por polillas)
que era una tierra frondosa,
donde junto a la ventura
se forjaban ardorosas proclamas.
Una comarca poblada de fértiles maderas,
aptas para el refugio de hombres, isópteros y orugas.
Y también para el fuego.

A Country

When the foreigner arrived
everyone had already left.

They say all he had in his hands
were watercolors by children who painted a country
where the texture of snow was scarcely imagined.

A place dreamed up by the cunning
and the customs of the light,
that naïvely held on to hiding spots
so the shadows could commit treason,
since before they were born.

Their innocent drawings
(now devoured by moths)
tell of an overgrown land
where along with good fortune
ardent proclamations were forged.
A region full of fertile forests,
an apt refuge for men, termites and larvae.
And also for fire.

La gente invisible

When you have city eyes you cannot see
the invisible people.

SALMAN RUSHDIE

Alguien debe recoger los muertos:
los de antes, los de ahora, los de siempre.
Alguien debe hacerlo.

Son urgentes la amnesia,
las calles limpias
y las flores en las aceras.

Tal vez sea la gente invisible
quien se ocupe de ellos.

Gente que al caminar
apenas deje huellas.

Gente sin padres ni abuelos.
Gente que está por nacer
y vendrá con aguaceros.

La gente invisible sabe cantar
pero prefiere el silencio,
sabe reír si corresponde
pero no se deja tentar por quimeras.

La gente invisible procura
hacer todo invisible,
lo que vemos y lo que no.

The Invisible People

*When you have city eyes you cannot see
the invisible people.*

SALMAN RUSHDIE

Someone has to collect the dead:
from before, from now, from always.
Someone has to do it.

We urgently need amnesia,
clean streets,
and flowers by the sidewalks.

Maybe the invisible people
are the ones who take care of them.

People who hardly leave
footprints when they walk.

People without parents or grandparents.
People who have yet to be born
and who'll come in a downpour.

The invisible people can sing
but they prefer silence,
they can laugh when appropriate
but they're untempted by illusions.

The invisible people try
to make everything invisible,
what we see and what we don't.

Por eso si alguien se los lleva serán ellos.
Para que las calles queden limpias,
sin sangre ni recuerdos.

So, if someone takes away the dead, it must be them.
So the streets remain clean,
with no blood and no memories.

CONFESSIONAL

CONFESIONARIO

Si me permites

Si me permites
no te llamaré por tu nombre,
procuraré otros atajos
que me sepan conducir
al sitio donde las palabras amanecen,
al recodo donde las historias
se reconocen inútiles
y el azar pacta
a riesgo de sus mejores apuestas.

Si me permites
te desearé simplemente
como si invocara la lluvia
en la estación más seca,
aquélla que queda
sin balbuceos
más allá de la aridez
del recuerdo
de lo que no fue.

Si me permites,
si hay un lugar donde yo pueda,
me haré hábito en tu piel
y como un devoto feligrés,
fiel a los caprichos del deseo
te haré mía sin nombres
sin palabras, sin promesas.

If You Let Me

If you let me
I won't call you by your name,
I'll seek out other shortcuts
that can lead me
to the place where words come up,
to the turns where stories
understand that they're useless
and chance concurs
at risk of its best bets.

If you let me
I'll want you simply
as if I were crying out
for rain in the driest season,
rain that stays
without a stutter
beyond the dryness
of the memory
of what wasn't.

If you let me,
if there's a place where I can,
I'll make myself a habit on your skin
and like a good churchgoer,
faithful to the whims of desire,
I'll make you mine with no names,
no words, no promises.

Interludio en altamar

Tras cada naufragio
las olas intrigan a nuestros cuerpos
y los acercan
como dos leños
que flotan
juntos,
sin ataduras,
para fundar una ínsula extraña,
perdida,
lejana,
un islote a la deriva
que no registren los mapas,
escondido en altamar.

High Seas Interlude

After every shipwreck
the waves intrigue our bodies
and bring them closer
like two bits of driftwood
that float
together,
untethered,
to found a strange isle,
lost,
distant,
a drifting islet
unmarked on maps,
hidden on the high seas.

Del lado de allá

Del otro lado,
de esa otra parte,
sospecho colinas que no dejan llegar el viento.

Allí no se conoce
la humedad,
solo ecos
y áridas voces,
la inveterada costumbre de hablar
siempre de cara al desierto.

Over There

On the other side,
somewhere else,
I imagine hills that don't let in the wind.

There, no one knows
moisture,
only echoes
and dry voices,
the inveterate habit of talking,
always facing the desert.

La espera

Si bien en lontananza aún te acecho
CARLOS GERMÁN BELLI

Aunque no me alcances
te esperaré.

Mientras no puedas
me mantendré en las sombras,
evadiré a los verdugos,
usaré sus capuchas,
cortaré con mi hacha
    en el sitio indicado
(un trazo limpio y sin dolor).

No tardaré en aprender mi oficio.

Mientras no puedas
cultivaré la paciencia,
me exiliaré en las promesas.

Pero tal vez tarde, al ras de nunca,
quizás a años de aquí, he de arrepentirme.

Y entonces como un ave cetrera
entrenada para herir y matar
dejaré mi capirote y volaré alto
hasta alcanzarte y hacerte mi presa,
o dejarte a lo lejos, junto al recuerdo,
junto a cuerpos malogrados y cadalsos.

The Wait

Even from afar, I come for you.
CARLOS GERMÁN BELLI

Even if you don't catch up to me,
I'll wait for you.

As long as you can't
I'll stay in the shadows,
I'll avoid the executioners,
I'll use their hoods,
I'll cut with my axe
      on the indicated spot
(a clean and painless stroke).

I won't take long to learn my trade.

As long as you can't
I'll cultivate patience,
I'll exile myself in promises.

But maybe late, flush with never,
perhaps years from now, I'll have to repent.

And then like a falconer's bird
trained to maim and kill
I'll shed my hood and I'll fly high
until I catch up to you and make you my prey,
or leave you in the distance, beside the memory,
beside spoiled bodies and gallows.

Entre manos

Cada mano se reconoce en la otra.
Recogidas sobre sí
encierran entre sus dedos
una difícil hermandad.
Extendidas, son francas,
serenas como mentiras encanecidas.
Cuando se juntan para rezar
imploran por el alivio de los rencores.
Si a la par confabulan
—pactan y palpan—
se reparten las caricias
de un único cuerpo,
el que da forma a sus deseos.
Juntas tantean un misterio venturoso.
Se reconocen y comercian con la eternidad.

Between Hands

Each hand recognizes itself in the other.
Folded in on themselves
they enclose between their fingers
a difficult brotherhood.
Extended, they are frank,
serene like graying lies.
When they come together to pray
they beg for an end to resentment.
Meanwhile, if they conspire
—make pacts and touch—
they distribute the caresses
of a single body,
the one that shapes their desires.
Together they feel about a fortunate mystery.
They recognize each other and do business with eternity.

Amor cósmico

Ya usted me sabrá disculpar,
pero le confieso que en materia de romances cósmicos
soy más bien incrédulo.

No vislumbro el amor de los astros
más allá de esas obligaciones
precavidamente contraídas con la gravedad.

No profeso el erotismo entre estelas planetarias
ni el fugaz apareamiento de las constelaciones.

Pues el amor, me parece, es una pesquisa
de cuerpos terrestres, de olores,
de tactos acordados en la mirada.

Un asunto sin trasuntos,
infiel a toda copia.

Un pacto de solitarios
que juntos lidian con estar aquí.

Y en la Tierra
soy creyente de la pasión.

Cosmic Love

You'll be kind enough to forgive me
when I confess that when it comes to cosmic romance
I'm somewhat incredulous.

I don't discern the sentiments of the stars
beyond their cautiously contractual
obligations to gravity.

I don't see comets as erotic
nor do I notice when the constellations mate.

And love, it seems to me, is a study
in terrestrial bodies, in odors,
in touches remembered from sight.

An irreplicable item,
resisting any copy.

A deal between solitary souls
that cope together with being here.

And on Earth
I'm a believer in passion.

La mujer imaginada

Una mujer imaginada en los andenes
de cualquier estación del metro de esta ciudad.
Una mujer que no llegó, que no vino
y sin embargo camina entre la gente
buscando las mismas salidas que nosotros.

Una mujer imaginada, perdida
en el bosque de Chapultepec
o en la espesura de algún sueño.

Una mujer imaginada, simplemente,
huyendo como todas ellas
de alguna foto que nadie ha tomado aún.

Ellas nos acompañan sin saberlo,
sin siquiera imaginarlo.

Por ellas caminamos junto a ellas
sobre las mismas accidentadas aceras
o pisamos hojas imaginadas, tal vez ya pisadas
por ellas, que apenas insinúan la existencia del otoño.

The Imagined Woman

An imagined woman on the platform
of any metro station in this city.
A woman who did not arrive, who didn't come
but nonetheless walks among the people
searching for the same exits as us.

An imagined woman, lost
in the forest of Chapultepec
or in the thickness of some dream.

An imagined woman, simply,
running away like all of them
from some photo no one has taken yet.

They walk with us but don't know it,
they don't even imagine it.

We walk beside them, on their behalf,
on the same uneven pavements
or step on imagined leaves, perhaps already stepped on
by them, who hardly insinuate the existence of the fall.

Amantes en tránsito

Se besan y cuando se besan
son como las adormideras.

Un opio denso los estremece.

En las esquinas:
lenguas y labios.
En los vagones:
caricias, lenguas y labios
En ascensores:
lenguas, labios, deseos.

Sin tregua hacen el amor
al pie de las escaleras.

Devotos al tacto,
envueltos en sí mismos
impúdicos en la pública vía,
se ponen así, sin ya querer despertar,
como las adormideras.

Lovers in Transit

They kiss and when they kiss
they're like poppies.

A dense opium makes them tremble.

On the corner:
tongues and lips.
In the train cars:
touches, tongues and lips
In elevators:
tongues, lips, desires.

They make relentless love
at the foot of the stairs.

Devoted to touch,
wrapped up in themselves,
shamelessly in public,
they lie there, not wanting to wake,
like poppies.

Al modo de Oliverio Girondo
(si hubiese sido mexicano)

Veinte millones de almas, hechas cuerpos,
se antojan, se huarachean, se alambran,
se aflautan, chilaquilean, se arracheran,
se tortillean, se enchilan, se emposolean,
se enmolan, se mixotean, se gusanean,
se enguacamolan, se enmolletean,
se enquesadillan, se fajitean,
se escamolean, se nopalean,
se agringan y al fin campechanean.

In the Style of Oliverio Girondo
(if he had been Mexican)

Twenty million souls, made bodies,
antojo each other, huarache each other, alambre each other,
flauta each other, chilaquil, arrachera each other,
tortilla each other, enchilada each other, pozole each other,
mole each other, mixote each other, gusano each other,
guacamole each other, mollete each other,
quesadilla each other, fajita each other,
escamol each other, nopal each other,
gringa each other and finally campechana.

Águilas nocturnas

Averiguo en la noche,
en la ambigüedad de los sueños:

Aguas congestionadas,
corrientes agolpadas en tuberías
y un estruendo periódico de aviones
que nadie sabe adónde van.

Tales son los signos que descifro
en este oscuro pentagrama.

Habito la latencia de un asombro primordial:

cuerpos desnudos, jadeantes,
leales a un ritmo cósmico,
aprendices de sagrados y ancestrales designios,
coronados por oráculos labrados
en las pirámides del Sol y la Luna.

Hilvano los sonidos que me rondan:

águilas nocturnas cruzan el cielo
danzando, en un rito, sobre aguas volcánicas.

Nocturnal Eagles

I find in the night,
in the ambiguity of dreams:

Congested waters,
currents clogged up in pipes
and an occasional boom from an airplane
going who knows where.

Such are the notes I decipher
on this dark staff.

I live in the latency of primordial wonder:

naked bodies, panting,
loyal to a cosmic rhythm,
apprentices of sacred and ancestral designs,
crowned by oracles carved
on the pyramids of the Sun and the Moon.

I link the sounds that surround me:

nocturnal eagles crisscross the sky,
dancing a rite over volcanic waters.

Amante cautivo (en Skype)

Hoy puedo verte
pero no tocarte.
Puedo conversar contigo,
siguiendo con mi dedo
la silueta de tu rostro.
Puedo amarte sin oler tu piel,
recorrerte a la distancia.
Besarte como un pez
confinado en su acuario,
rehaciendo recuerdos
que no provienen de la memoria
sino de espejos anegados
más allá, al otro lado,
al fondo de esta pantalla.

Lover Held Captive (in Skype)

Today I can see you
but not touch you.
I can talk to you,
tracing the silhouette
of your face with my finger.
I can love you without smelling your skin,
traverse you from a distance.
Kiss you like a fish
confined in an aquarium,
remaking moments
that come not from my memory
but from flooded mirrors
beyond, on the other side,
in the depths of this screen.

Escrito a deshora

En la lejanía se presienten urgentes
las muchas cartas debidas,
las muchas palabras detenidas
en la víspera de un indeciso adiós.

A cierta distancia los recuerdos
se aglomeran en oscuras playas
y abruptos se enfilan los palotes
de una caligrafía pautada
para cercar a la memoria

Pero escribir a destiempo,
contra el silencio,
no amaina tampoco
la obsesión por las tachaduras.

De haberse dicho antes,
de haberse dicho sin demoras,
tal vez, solo tal vez, toda escritura
se haría vana y hablaría el tiempo.

Written at the Wrong Time

From far away, the still-unwritten letters
take on a sense of urgency,
the countless words paused
on the precipice of an indecisive goodbye.

At a certain distance, moments
congregate on dark beaches
and, abruptly, the brushstrokes
of a neat calligraphy line up
to fence in memory.

But writing out of time,
against the silence,
does nothing to ease
the obsession with crossing out words.

Had it been said before,
had it been said without pause,
then maybe, just maybe, all writing
would be in vain and time would do the talking.

Escrito en la arena

Todo se hace diáfano,
tarde o temprano.

Dímelo de una vez.

No es necesario apartar la mirada
de las cosas simples
para abandonar lo que fue.

Uno podría demorarse en el borde
de los vasos cultivando el deseo silencioso
de distraer el terror a las despedidas.

Las olas, sin saber pensar,
borran y esconden en la arena
lo que hubo sin dejar lugar
a remordimientos.

Y ni aún el mejor de los navegantes
logra aplacar la voluntad de las mareas.

Written on the Sand

Everything becomes transparent
sooner or later.

Tell me once and for all.

We don't have to take our eyes
off the simple things
to abandon what was.

One could idle on the edge
of a glass, cultivating the silent desire
to distract the fear of goodbyes.

The waves, without thinking,
erase and cover up whatever was
on the sand, leaving no room
for regrets.

And not even the finest navigator
can alter the will of the tides.

Reencuentro

Tú y yo volveremos a encontrarnos
en una foto que no has tomado aún,
en un instante que ya fue
y todavía aguarda
por nosotros.

Reunion

You and I will find each other again
in a photo you haven't yet taken,
in an instant that already was
and that still waits
for us.

Mi vida

Déjame recordarte
avenida con un reloj de arena:

aplacada por un árido e incesante goteo,

vigilada gracias a una frágil muralla de cristal.

My Life

Let me remember you
reconciled with an hourglass:

soothed by a dry, incessant drip,

watched over thanks to a fragile wall of glass.

ANTEVERSUS

ANTEVERSUS

.

Poema

A la memoria de Miguel Hernández

Entre tú y yo están las palabras,
aquellas que dirimen sus silencios en secreto
pues no encuentran confidentes en otro lugar.

Entre nosotros está la vida,
esa trama de instantes indispuestos al olvido,
urdida contigo desde la soledad.

Están la gente, los días, las ventanas,
las pisadas y monedas anegadas en la lluvia.

Y está la muerte, esa noche de fallidos recodos,
donde moran, sin candiles, arrepentidas luciérnagas.

Están los que fuimos y partieron,
los recuerdos de indecisas cerraduras.

Y está el amor, piedra preciosa
desenterrada del vientre de un lecho
del que nacerán furtivas arboledas.

Entre tú y yo están las palabras,
Entre nosotros, poema, están la vida, la muerte y el amor.

Poem

In memory of Miguel Hernández

Between you and me are words,
those that settle their silences in secret
as they find no confidants anywhere else.

Between us is life,
a plot of instants not easily forgotten,
concocted with you in solitude.

There are people, days, windows,
footsteps and coins washed away in the rain.

And there is death, that night of missed turns,
where remorseful fireflies live with no light.

There are those who we were
and those who departed,
and memories of indecisive locks.

And there is love, a precious stone
dug up from the belly of a riverbed
where furtive groves of trees will grow.

Between you and me are words,
Between us, dear poem, are life, death, and love.

Poeta de tiempos nada risueños

Y después ríe
ríe sin sentido
JORGE TEILLIER

Al escribir
se reía,
su caligrafía resguardaba
el ritmo entrecortado
de una risa torcida.
Se reía,
lo hacía malamente.
No había motivo que aplacara su risa
mientras anotaba la crónica de sus días.
Sin ser espejo
solo eso en el papel se veía.
Se reía nerviosamente,
entre tics conjugaba su rictus
con crímenes y aluviones,
con causas perdidas,
con su falta de fe en las profecías.

Poet of Unsmiling Times

*And then he laughs
he laughs for no reason*
JORGE TEILLIER

As he wrote
he laughed,
his handwriting kept up
the staggered rhythm
of a crooked chuckle.
He laughed
with malice.
Nothing could appease his laughter
as he jotted down the chronicle of his days.
While not a mirror,
the page displayed only his laughter.
He laughed nervously,
between tics he conjugated his grimace
with crimes and downpours,
with lost causes,
with his lack of faith in prophecies.

La hormiga

Déjala volver a su hormiguero.

Si distraída toca tus dedos
sube por ellos
y en los surcos que le ofrece tu mano
se queda ausente,
no la ahuyentes ni la aplastes.

Déjala volver, como pueda, a su hormiguero.
Guíala al lugar que pertenece.

Ya las otras, socarronas, harán burla
de sus costumbres,
de su terca desorientación.

Déjala volver, si puede, a su hormiguero,
aunque no lleve ningún vestigio de hojas
en su lomo de hormiga

No la mates. Allí otras
siempre pocas, la acompañarán
y le darán sitio entre todas.

Quizás ella también
(como tú en el poema)
confunde sin soberbia
el misterio del mundo
con la palma de tu mano.

The Ant

Let it go back to the anthill.

If it brushes inattentively against your fingers
climbs them
and daydreams
in the furrows of your hand,
don't chase it away or squash it.

Let it go back, as best it can, to the anthill.
Guide it to where it belongs.

Surely the others, those smart-asses, will make fun
of its new habits,
of its stubborn disorientation.

Let it go back, if it can, to the anthill,
even though it carries no shred of a leaf
on its ant's back.

Don't kill it. There, others,
but not many, will welcome it
and find it a place in the crowd.

Maybe it
(just like you in the poem)
confuses, without hubris,
the mystery of the world
with the palm of your hand.

Cuidados intensivos

A la memoria de Wislawa Szymborska

Mis hermanos no leen poesía,
mis padres tampoco lo hicieron.
Por dictamen de estos tiempos
tal costumbre, ya familiar,
mis hijos la fortalecen en la escuela.

No obstante, toda cadena flaquea,
alguna vez, por su eslabón más débil.

Y entonces la poesía nos deja en evidencia:
señala con sorna un fatal padecimiento.

(También las palabras convalecen
bajo el asombro cotidiano).

Si hay conmiseración la lástima se abrevia.

Pero si el asunto se prolonga,
si adquiere largura la dolencia,
por tu bien, y la tranquilidad de los tuyos,
has de extremar otras unciones:

someter a cuidados intensivos el poema.

Intensive Care

In memory of Wislawa Szymborska

My siblings don't read poetry,
my parents didn't either.
By dictate of the present day
my children strengthen
this tradition, now familiar, at school.

Nonetheless, all chains grow loose,
sooner or later, at their weakest link.

And then poetry lays us bare:
it sarcastically reveals a fatal ailment.

(Words also convalesce
under everyday wonder.)

If there is commiseration, the pity is cut short.

But if the matter is prolonged,
if the malady stretches further,
for your own good and your people's peace
seek out other extreme unctions:

admit the poem to intensive care.

Pórtico

Diariamente la noche cultiva
una llanura blanca
                donde germinará el poema.

Presiente su brote
         atenta
                al paso de las estaciones.

Quizás lo haga en otoño.

También se florece a destiempo.

Portico

Every day, nighttime cultivates
a flat white plot
                in which to plant the poem.

It senses the sprouts,
        attentive
                to the passing of the seasons.

Maybe it'll come in by the fall.

Sometimes flowers bloom at the wrong time.

La custodia

No sé dónde ocurren los sueños,
por eso escribo.

Lo hago como un monje que evade
su incredulidad y reza con fe ciega,
a contra mano, acorralado
entre la oscuridad y el silencio.

Mi tarea es excavar inciertos poemas,
trazar túneles y pasadizos
con la esperanza de alcanzar espléndidas galerías.

Soy, o quisiera ser, el hijo expósito
de una Orden Templaria extinta y olvidada.

No vislumbro en las noches el Santo Grial.

Sin embargo, insisto,
busco enmendar su custodia,
guarecer
        el cauce de los sueños.

Por eso escribo.

The Reliquary

I don't know where dreams take place,
that's why I write.

I write like a monk who denies
his incredulity and prays with blind faith,
one hand against the other, cloistered
between darkness and silence.

My task is to excavate unknown poems,
to dig tunnels and passageways
in the hope of stumbling into splendid galleries.

I am, or I'd like to be, the orphan son
of an extinct, forgotten order of Templars.

At night I catch no glimpse of the Holy Grail.

Nevertheless, I persist,
I seek to repair its reliquary,
to keep watch
        over the source of dreams.

That's why I write

Advertencia

Y ahora las palabras
no son más palabras
y las cosas no están
ni dentro ni fuera de ellas,
están donde no hay palabras
que tampoco es un lugar que tenga nombre.

Warning

And now words
are no longer words
and things are not
within them or outside them,
they are where there are no words
which is a place that has no name.

Una antigua historia de amantes

Inventar una palabra,
devenir en ella,
poseerla
siempre de paso,
rodearla sin asedios,
de a poco,
sin previsión de asustarla.
Plantarse allí,
cultivarla,
pedirle frutos
ofrecerla en procura
de nuevas cosechas
pero siempre abandonarla.
Andar así
sin palabras
disponiendo de siempre
de nunca
como si en cada decir
un mismo ciclo
de vida y muerte se agotara,
un eterno volver,
después, antes, nada.

An Old Love Story

Invent a word,
become her,
possess her,
always briefly,
surround her peacefully,
bit by bit,
not hoping to scare her.
Plant yourself there,
cultivate her,
ask for her fruits
offer her in exchange
for new harvests
but always abandon her.
Carry on
without words
making use of always
of never
as if in everything that's said
the same cycle
of life and death ran its course,
an eternal coming back,
after, before, nothing.

Sin nada a cambio

Aunque no hubiera nada después,
escribiría.
Escribiría
aunque callaran los dogmas,
sin lápiz,
sin bitácora,
sin papel.
Escribiría
no para responder,
no para salvarme.

Nothing In Return

Even if nothing came after,
I would write.
I would write
even if all dogmas went quiet,
with no pencil,
no notebook,
no paper.
I would write
not to answer,
not to save myself.

Con poca luz

Uno está perdido
desde antes de nacer.
Toma una calle,
luego otra,
vislumbra una ciega
y al final pregunta.

Pero pocos saben
lo que tampoco uno.

Si es de noche
presentimos
la víspera de algo,
tal vez un cauce definitivo.

Si no pasa nada
y amanece
nos encerramos
en una habitación con poca luz,
para escribir sobre la noche
y la gente perdida en ella,
calle tras calle, hasta el crepúsculo.

With Little Light

We are lost
before we're born.
We go down one street,
then another,
we spot a blind woman at a dead end
and eventually we ask.

But few know
what we don't.

If it's nighttime,
we sense
something coming,
perhaps a definitive course.

If nothing happens
and the sun rises
we shut ourselves up
in a room with little light,
to write about the night
and the people lost in it,
street after street, until dusk.

WATERING HOLE

ABREVADERO

*

Las ideas son peces que arrastramos en una red, tal vez esa que llamamos lenguaje. Para que sigan vivas debemos devolverlas al agua. Luego, más crecidas, habremos de atraparlas y liberarlas nuevamente. A veces cedemos a la tentación de comerlas. Alimentarnos en exceso de ellas las coloca (y nos coloca) en peligro de extinción.

*

Para expresar una idea no basta hallar las palabras adecuadas a ella. Hay que hallar en las palabras la idea que deseamos expresar.

*

La escritura no es anterior a las palabras, no obstante desde siempre estuvo en su interior, esperando germinar.

*

*Desde lejos
el mar y el cielo,
un azul extendido
donde nubes y olas
averiguan
cómo escribir
en un idioma donde nada se aquieta.*

*

Toda idea de Dios que dependa de las palabras es atea.

*

Ideas are fish that we dredge up in a net, maybe the net we
call language. To keep them alive we have to return them to
the water. Later, when they've matured, we have to trap
them and let them go again. Sometimes we give in to
temptation and eat them. Consuming them in excess puts
them (and us) in danger of extinction.

*

To express an idea, it's not enough to find the right words for
it. We have to find, in the words, the idea that we want to
express.

*

Writing doesn't come before words, but nonetheless it has
always been within them, waiting to germinate.

*

From afar
the sea and the sky,
an extended blue
where clouds and waves
find out
how to write
in a language where nothing settles.

*

Any idea of God that depends on words is atheistic.

*

Como toda forma de vida las palabras luchan por sobrevivir.
Viven intentando demorar su sepultura en los diccionarios.

*

La tradición ha hecho de la emoción un atributo del corazón.
Aunque otros ven allí sólo una máquina armoniosa donde conviven
sístoles y diástoles, movimientos esdrújulos, opuestos a la agudeza
de la razón.

*

El sentido,
sí,
el sentido,
siempre que persista
debajo
el latido.

*

En el dolor
se maceran palabras
que jamás serán escritas.

Sobre ellas escribimos sin saberlo.

*

Aprender a escuchar el silencio. No hacer silencio sin escuchar.

*

Like any life form, words fight to survive. They live their
lives attempting to hold off their burial in dictionaries.

*

Tradition tells us that emotion is an attribute of the heart.
However, others only see a harmonious machine of
coexisting systoles and diastoles, strangely accented
movements, opposed to the acuity of reason.

*

Meaning,
yes,
but feeling
as long as it stays
beneath
what's beating.

*

In pain
steep words
that will never be written.

We write over them without knowing.

*

Learn to listen to silence. Don't make silence without
listening.

*

Las ideas y las nubes
tienen un evidente parentesco.
Ambas flotan
    y se desplazan
hasta convertirse
            en otra cosa,
        al caer
bajo el influjo
de la gravedad
terrestre.

*

De ser verbo
resistiría el vértigo.

Vería el mundo en reposo
sobre dos alas
            adormecidas.

Contemplaría desde lo alto
las piedras
en su caída,
        ya fatigadas del ascenso,
        cansadas del vano intento
                de volar.

*

Nada digo
al decir
que al decir
"digo"
ya dije

*

Ideas and clouds
are clearly related.
They both float
    and move about
until they turn
        into something else
    as they fall
under the influence
of terrestrial
gravity.

*

If I were a verb
I would resist vertigo.

I would see the world, gliding
on two still
        wings.

From high up I would contemplate
the stones
as they fell,
    fatigued from their ascent,
    tired from their vain attempt
            to fly.

*

I say nothing
when I say
that when I say
"I say"
I already said

*

En el mismo aire
del que se alimenta el fuego
conspira el soplido
que lo ha de extinguir.

*

Casi toda certeza
es un calabozo.

Dudar, nuestra condena.

*

No me acompaño
de verdades.

Trato de guarecerme
en esa zona
húmeda
donde las ideas
corretean
desnudas,
voltean
y se hunden
sin ofrecernos
nada a cambio.

*

La verdad, ah, esa dama de pies ligeros.

*

With the same oxygen
that feeds the flame
conspires the gust of air
that blows it out.

*

Almost every certainty
is a prison cell.

To doubt, our sentence.

*

I don't associate
with truths.

I try to take shelter
in that wetland
where ideas
walk around
naked,
flip over
and sink,
offering us
nothing in return.

*

Truth, oh yes, that lady who's light on her feet.

*

Al contrario de lo que piensas, las ideas van de su cuenta. Se saludan para compartir rumores pero nunca olvidan las prebendas de su linaje. Sin atenuantes, sin falsa compasión, se burlan de las palabras, las traicionan y las entregan como Judas al mejor (im) postor.

*

Creo que no creo. Tan solo escribo sin copia del original.

*

Poeta contemporáneo: constructor de ruinas frescas para el gozo de los arqueólogos del porvenir.

*

*Un lenguaje que encubra
(y descubra)
sin hacerse notar,
que oculte
(y revele)
con sigilo.*

*Un arte de lo mínimo
(o con una m menos, de lo nimio),
en el que sin excesos
se haga sentir
el cartílago de la lengua.*

*

Contrary to what you think, ideas get by on their own. They greet each other to share rumors but they never forget the privileges of their rank. Without extenuating circumstances, without false compassion, they mock words, betray them, and hand them over like Judas to the highest bidder (or the best pretender).

*

I believe I do not create. I just write without a copy of the original.

*

Contemporary poet: builder of fresh ruins for the enjoyment of future archaeologists.

*

A language that covers up
(and uncovers)
without making itself obvious,
that hides
(and reveals)
with discretion.

An art of the minimal
(or, changing the consonants, of the trivial)
in which, without excess,
one can feel
the cartilage of the tongue.

*

TODO POEMA ES UN PALIMPSESTO:

una respuesta   *a una pregunta*
                        que desconocemos
                                debajo
                          de lo escrito

*

En estos tiempos, como los pacientes de cuidado, también las palabras.

*

EVERY POEM IS A PALIMPSEST:

a response   to a question
                    we don't know
                        below
                    what's written

*

These days, like patients in care, also words.

I. In early 2007, I traveled fourteen hours across country with my friend, the Chilean poet Marcelo Rioseco, from Cincinnati, on the banks of the Ohio River, to New York City. The main motive of this short visit to Manhattan, which lasted just three days, was to attend a retrospective exhibition of the works of the Venezuelan painter Armando Reverón, which was then about to close in the city's Museum of Modern Art.

Almost a year later, on February 5, 2008, back in Cincinnati, I wrote an email to Eugenio Montejo in which I mentioned his last message and mine before it, copied to Pedro Lastra, together with a poem called "Reverón, Macuto-New York (MoMA 2007)," which I dedicated to them both. Part of my message said the following: "a few days ago I tried several times to send you an email thanking you for the extraordinary poem by Supervielle and the translation by Paz, along with a poem I wrote a while ago that I dedicated to you and Pedro. The message wouldn't send several times, so I don't know if it reached you in the end or not. I've just received one from Pedro that I'd like to share with you, along with a copy of the poem I mentioned." Pedro Lastra's message, dated from that same day, acknowledged receipt of the letter I sent by mail the week before and evoked the circumstances implied by the poem as well as the strange synchronicity manifested at the moment of receiving my message. Pedro put it like this: "I've received your lovely poem about Reverón, dedicated to Eugenio and myself: I was moved by the poem and the thought of that memorable outing to Macuto. The footprints we left there are still recorded in some photographs. But there is something, Arturo, 'which certainly is not defined / by the word fate...': It is this: on Saturday, Rigas Kappatos visited me from Maryland and stayed at my house. On Sunday morning he noticed the photo that Anita took of us, Eugenio and me, in Reverón's house, surrounded by his canvases and dolls. Since we were with him at the MoMA exhibition back in 2007, I was telling him about that outing, and we talked for a long time about Reverón... And yesterday morning I received what you sent..." The outing to which Pedro referred took place in January of 1999. At that time, while he was passing through Caracas, on Eugenio's initiative we organized a visit to Reverón's Castillete in Macuto. Pedro and his granddaughter, along with Eugenio, our families, and myself, shared that afternoon rummaging around and exploring the quarters where Armando Reverón lived, building his illusory world and refuge among peculiar objects, dolls, canvases, animals, the wind, and the sound of the palm trees. Several photos provide evidence of that afternoon. Photos that, as Pedro Lastra himself said elsewhere, offer a "fleeting sensation of irreality," since with the devastating passage of time and the tragic landslide that took place at the end of that same year, they acquired the quality not only of privileged testimonies but also of enigmatic signs, and perhaps premonitions.

In Eugenio's response, sent to me on February 6, 2008, he offers a reading of the poem that alludes to this sensation. He says the following: "Pedro's message is full of affection, with his typical hint of something hidden. The coincidence that he spoke about the photo from the Castillete shortly before receiving the poem is itself a sure indication that something connects all these apparent coincidences. The poem has the tone of a Renaissance elegy, like Rodrigo Caro's 'A las ruinas de Itálica' or Joachim du Bellay's sonnet 'A Roma,' imitated and much improved upon by Quevedo. The question of what remains of a place, of a fond memory."

Perhaps these "apparent coincidences" are the result of a preexisting desire to seek out associations. In his message, Eugenio speaks in detail about the illness he had been suffering since the previous October, the medical tests he'd taken to dispel his doubts, and how his fears seemed to be relieved "for the moment." Unfortunately, this was not so, and four months later he had to depart, leaving us, as he said in his message, with the "question of what remains" and the nostalgia of his "fond memory."

II. Marcos Camacho, better known as "Marcola," is the leader of a criminal organization in São Paulo, Brazil called the Primeiro Comando da Capital (PCC). This poem is constructed using Marcola's own words, taken from an interview in the newspaper *O Globo*.

CONTENTS

𝒜

INTENSIVE CARE | ARTURO GUTIÉRREZ PLAZA

Made in Miami Beach ~ Printing as needed

◊◊◊

2020

www.ingramcontent.com/pod-product-compliance
Lightning Source LLC
Chambersburg PA
CBHW020154090426
42734CB00008B/820